TaKe iT FROM HERe!

GLEE YODER
SUGGESTIONS FOR CreaTive acTiviTies

Page Layout by Linda Beher

JUDSON PRESS, Valley Forge

TAKE IT FROM HERE

Copyright ©1973
Judson Press, Valley Forge, PA 19481

Except where otherwise indicated, the Bible quotations in this volume are in accordance with the Revised Standard Version of the Bible, copyright © 1946 and 1954, by the Division of Christian Education of the National Council of the Churches of Christ in the United States of America, and are used by permission.

Also used is *Today's English Version of the New Testament*. Copyright © American Bible Society, 1966. Used by permission. (Marked "TEV" following reference.)

Library of Congress Cataloging in Publication Data
Yoder, Glee.
   Take it from here.
    1. Creative activities and seat work. 2. Religious education. I. Title.
BV1536.Y63   268'.6   72-9570
ISBN 0-8170-0584-6

Printed in the U.S.A.

ACKNOWLEDGMENTS

Messenger magazine has graciously granted permission to reprint the following units which first appeared as articles under the title "Take It from Here" in that magazine: "Press a Bolt Here, a Paper Clip There,"* "Bread Is for Breaking,"* "A Humdrummer for a Humdrum Day,"* "Rubbings Revived,"* "A Matter of Circles,"* "Making Some Unusual Slides,"* "Tissues—Not for Blowing but for Dipping,"* "Fly with a Banner,"* "No Two Faces Alike," "Nature's Own Paint and Beads,"* "Tie Them in Knots,"* "In and Out with Soda Straws," "Fun with Words,"* "Poetry for Thanksgiving,"* "What to Do on the Road,"* and "The Eyes Have It." Mr. Wilbur Brumbaugh of the staff of *Messenger* worked with Linda Beher on the layout of the units marked with an * in the above list. Don Honick of the *Messenger* staff took the photographs on pages 7, 17, 43, 57, and 59. The photographs on pages 46 and 63 were taken by Edward J. Buzinski, also a member of the *Messenger* staff. Art work was done by *Messenger* staff people as follows: Linda Beher on pages 8, 19, 25, and 59; Wilbur Brumbaugh the rubbing on page 17; Bridget Burren the macrame on pages 44 and 45; Ken Stanley the art work on pages 20, 21, 54, 55, and 60; and Stan Whipple the sculpture pictured on page 57. R. Gordon Yoder supplied the photographs that appear on page 18.

Permission has been received for use of other photographs as follows:

Gene Ahrens on page 41;[3]

American Research Photography on page 22;[1]

Clark and Clark on pages 6 and 49;[4]

A. Devaney, Inc. on page 14;

Rohn Engh on page 32;[2]

Richard Harrington on page 34;

Larry Kitzel on pages 27, 30, 31, 33, 35, 37, 38, 39, 47, 49,[4] and 51;

Henry Long on page 8;

H. Armstrong Roberts on pages 40, 41,[3] and 55;

Tom Stack and Associates on pages 19, 25, 32,[2] and 56;

Edward Wallowitch for photographs on pages 9, 10, 11, 13, 22,[1] 26, 42, 50, 58, and 62.

Permission for the use of quoted material has been received from the following:

From Abingdon Press for the poem on page 53 by Elizabeth Allstrom from *You Can Teach Creatively,* Copyright © 1970 by Abingdon Press.

From Earle W. Fike for the poem which appears on page 9.

From Harcourt Brace Jovanovich, Inc., for the use on page 52 of one line from the poem "Fog" by Carl Sandburg from *Complete Poems of Carl Sandburg* published by Harcourt Brace Jovanovich, Inc.

From Harper and Row, Publishers, for quotation on page 58 from Dietrich Bonhoeffer, *Life Together* (New York: Harper and Row, Publishers, 1954), pp. 42 and 43.

From Judson Press for quotation on page 24 from Clarence Jordan, *Sermon on the Mount* (Valley Forge: Judson Press, 1952), p. 68 of Koinonia Edition.

From Corita Kent for the use on page 8 of a quotation from *Headlines and Footnotes.*

From W. W. Norton & Company, Inc., for quotations on page 62 from Robert Paul Smith, *Where Did You Go? Out. What Did You Do? Nothing.,* Copyright © 1957 by Robert Paul Smith.

From Random House, Inc., for quotation on page 24 of one line from *The Sound of Music* by Howard Lindsay and Russel Crouse.

[1] Page 22, photographs of young adults and old woman by Wallowitch, of the young boy by American Research Photography.

[2] Page 32, photograph of the old man by Rohn Engh, of boy by Tom Stack and Associates.

[3] Page 41, photograph of the tree by Gene Ahrens, of daisies by H. Armstrong Roberts.

[4] Page 49, photograph of carving by Larry Kitzel, of the woman by Clark and Clark.

CONTENTS

press a bolt here, a paper clip there

"Experiences are the stuff from which concepts grow, and experiences are man's reaching out to see and hear, to smell and taste, to touch the environment of persons and things in which he finds himself, and becomes involved," writes Kathrene Tobey in *Learning and Teaching Through the Senses.*

Each person has his *own* center of experience from which he reaches out to take from his environment what *he* needs. Such experiences, varied and abundant, make for a wholeness that comes from full, active living, including a dream of something which is one's very own — something for which there are no kits, no plastic molds, or even rules of thumb.

In our society it takes courage to be creative because creativity means thinking and acting independently. It often means following an urge or a "glimpse" which seems impractical in terms of our everydayness. In a day of quick-drying, speed-reading, and instant perfection we rely on fast and sure things, end results which we can see readily and which we know will conform to present "standards of excellence." It is a long way from the slow, sure development that comes from living with materials and gradually associating form and idea. The woman who cleaned the wool, carded it, spun it into yarn, and knit from it a sweater felt her materials and envisioned in each step the forming of her own creation. A farmer, even today, cultivates a feel for his fields and animals and weather. He associates and learns by gradually putting together what he discovers about a given object or condition, tests this information as he goes along, sees parts within the whole, generalizes, and evaluates. He goes by the feel of things and conditions.

Bernard Leach, in *A Potter's Book,* reports that when a master Japanese potter was asked how a person could recognize good work, the answer was, "With his body." It must feel right to *him.* With his mind acting directly through his senses he gains an impression through his own personal experience of use and beauty combined.

Keeping in mind the Japanese potter's advice, try the two activities which are suggested. They capture not only the feel of the outer planes of a surface but also the full three-dimensional form of relief. Look for materials through which you can experience the touching-feeling process of round and flat, smooth and rough, delicate and coarse, sharp and dull, concave and convex. Spools, bolts, hair curlers, bottle caps, rough pieces of wood, shells, seed pods, machine parts, and cardboard tubes are some of the materials you may find.

A second experiment uses the cylinder rolls of waxed paper, aluminum foil, and toilet tissue; drinking straws; various sizes of paper cups. The base of the relief is a plastic foam tray on which prepackaged meat is wrapped.

In one process the relief surface is pressed into a small slab of soft clay to make a three-dimensional imprint. The clay surface may be scraped flat again and again, so do a lot of experimenting. The trying-out stage needs to be sheer fun until out of the "I like that" experience there begins to develop an arrangement or composition which satisfies you.

It is usually rewarding for the materials to be varied and associated with other imprints by overlapping, reappearing, continuing, and varying the depth of the imprints.

To plan the design cut paper the size of the meat tray. Cut the rolls into various lengths and place the cylinders in an arrangement which is pleasing to you. Try placing small tubes inside larger ones. Tall ones coming out of short ones. Interlocking some.

Pour plaster of Paris into the plastic meat tray to a thickness of ⅛" to ¼". Transfer the design on the paper, piece by piece, to the meat tray by pressing the tubes in the plaster. Allow the plaster to set up, then remove the tray from the base. Color may be added if desired (see above) and clay may be used instead of plaster of Paris.

Using the imprinted clay as a mold, one may pour plaster of Paris to make a cast. To do this, add a clay wall to the slab by rolling out a clay strip that will go around the slab and high enough to stand about an inch above its surface. A wire or paper clip set in the wet plaster will provide for hanging. After the plaster has set (about a half hour) remove the clay mold and wash the plaster cast.

Since your imprint does not capture color, study these forms in their new state and relationship to see whether the effect might be enhanced by adding color. Using poster paints or water colors, with small brushes, try painting parts of your relief.

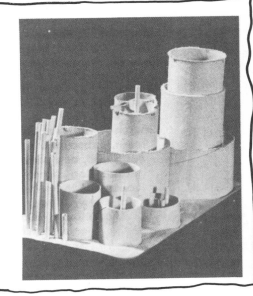

BREAD IS FOR BREAKING

"Don't touch!"

"Don't put in your mouth!"

But Jesus said, "Take, eat. . . ." He took the bread, blessed it, broke it, and shared it with his disciples. The Bible is full of experiences in which the senses played an important role in the building and strengthening of relationships between persons. Jesus opened the ears of the deaf and they heard; he restored sight to the blind and they saw. He touched the hand of the leper and immediately he was clean again. They touched the fringe of his garment and as many as touched it were made well.

How refreshing cool water felt to tired, dusty feet! How soothing the oil gently rubbed into the wounds of the man left bleeding beside the road! How fragrant the ointment poured on the head of Jesus! The senses are marvelous avenues of response to one's neighbor and to God, his world, and his creatures.

Who can forget the aroma of a loaf of bread as it is taken from the oven? Rich, firm bread, with a thick crust, made from good wholesome grain. It is so common, so universal, yet so needed, so nourishing. In it is seedtime and harvest, labor and love, hope and fulfillment — life itself! It is said that a hasty man will cut it with a knife but a man who loves food and life does bread the honor of breaking

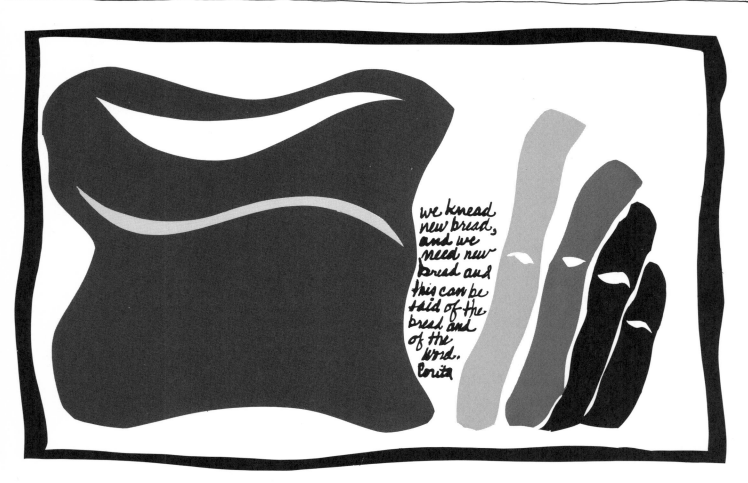

we knead new bread, and we need new bread and this can be said of the bread and of the Word. Corita

it with his hands.

So they broke it in a communion service. One participant expressed her feelings in this way: "I took the small loaf from the basket and broke off a chunk. I was aware of its freshness, the fine texture of its center. I noted the many varieties in the basket before I passed it to the worshiper next to me. While some of the loaves were topped with seeds, my piece was quite unadorned — simply a scarred crust covering a finely textured center. It smelled sweet. This was one of those rare moments of worship when the secular and sacred meet, or perhaps when the secular becomes sacred. 'Give us this day our daily bread.' 'Man lives not by bread alone.' 'Take, eat; this is my body.' 'I am the Bread of Life.' These thoughts ran through my mind. . . . We saw; we heard; we smelled; we touched; we tasted. Through that celebration, the daily had become special; the secular had become sacred."

A participant in a chitterling communion service wrote of their breaking cracklin' cornbread together.

It was a party to welcome in the New Year, a communion supper with a special "black meal" menu—the first time "soul" food had dominated the communion dinner at that church in Chicago. Some wondered if it might have been the first "soul" communion in that particular denomination. "As we broke fresh, warm cornbread with cracklings and spoke of the breaking of bread together in the promised body of Christ."

Another church celebrated worldwide communion with traditional breads from many countries. Women of the congregation baked the kinds of breads their mothers or grandmothers had baked from "old country" recipes or from recipes which their own families especially enjoyed. Hungarian, Chinese, Dutch, Swedish, German, English, Mexican, Navajo, and others — breads of the world — helped the congregation to feel truly a part of the world family of man who remember "the bread which we break is the communion of the body of Christ."

THE PEACE IS GIVEN

Some Asian churches have a unique form of benediction which is being used by some American congregations. At the close of the worship when the peace is given, all take part. The giver places his right hand against the right palm of the receiver, and each closes the left hand over the other's right. The giver says in a low voice, "The peace of God be with you." The receiver then turns to the person next to him and gives the peace to him. In a larger congregation the leader gives it to the first person in each pew who will then pass it on to the next person. In this tactual experience persons can feel truly "members one of another" as they speak God's blessing.

Lord,
    You are always doing miracles with common things.
    You give us
        the nurture of the earth
        the sprout of the seed
        grain
        the skill of an unknown baker
            and we share the goodness of bread;
            but the miracle of how bread comes to us is hidden from us.
    You give this bread, Lord, a common thing.
    We eat, and share in its goodness;
        but the miracle of how life in Jesus Christ is given is hidden from us.
    As we eat, help us to share in the miracle and rejoice in the reality of Jesus Christ. Amen.
                    (Earle W. Fike Jr.)

"Seven out of every ten minutes that you and I are conscious, alive and awake we are communicating verbally in one of its forms; and that communication time is devoted 9 per cent to writing; 16 per cent to reading, 30 per cent to speaking, and 45 per cent to listening." So reported Dr. Paul Rankin after an extensive study. Yet experiments show that we listen at only a 25 per cent level of efficiency when listening to a ten-minute speech. How inefficient we are in doing the thing we do most frequently all our lives—listening!

If really to be heard, really to be taken seriously, is every man's basic need, as some psychologists believe, how little help we must be to those with whom we associate day after day. I am reminded of what Dietrich Bonhoeffer wrote in *Life Together*:

Many people are looking for an ear that will listen. They do not find it among Christians, because these Christians are talking where they should be listening. But he who can no longer listen to his brother will soon be no longer listening to God either; he will be doing nothing but prattle in the presence of God too.

TAKE OFF THOSE EAR- MUFFS!

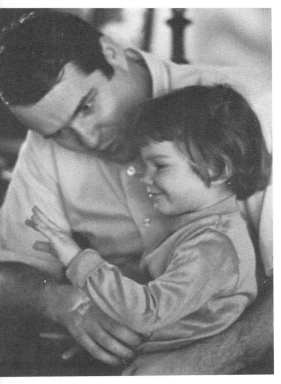

TAKE OFF THOSE EARMUFFS!

Learning through listening is an "inside" job. The listener must replace some of his common present attitudes with more positive ones. Ralph G. Nichols suggests ten guides to good listening:

1. Ask yourself, "What is he saying that can be of help to me—in facts or in learning to know him better? What worthwhile ideas does he have?" G. K. Chesterton once said, "There is no such thing as an uninteresting subject; there are only uninterested people."

2. Judge content, not package. The message is ten times more important than the who or how. Mannerisms are quickly forgotten when you become interested in the subject.

3. Hold your fire. Withhold evaluation until you are certain you understand what the person is really saying.

4. Listen for the central idea—the gist of what the other person is saying.

5. Summarize. Listen for three minutes and then make a mental summary. You can't remember everything that has been said.

6. Work at listening. It is hard work. Establish eye contact and maintain it. You help not only yourself but you also will help the other person to express himself better.

7. Resist distractions. Good listening is a matter of concentration.

8. Exercise your mind. Develop an anticipation for hearing ideas which are difficult enough to challenge your mental capacities.

9. Keep your mind open. "Deaf spots," evoking an emotional reaction, cause your communication efficiency to drop to zero.

10. Capitalize on thought speed. Most persons talk at the rate of 125 words a minute. We can think *four* times that fast. Learn to use this spare thinking time to summarize, to listen between the lines, and to weigh the ideas presented.

GIVING AND TAKING

All conversation can be thought of in terms of giving and taking. Both giving and taking can be done while either talking or listening. Giving through talking is done when one gives information, advice, or praise, or when sharing one's feelings and experiences with others. Giving is done through listening when one gives one's time and attention to the other person's expressions.

Taking in talking is when one expresses one's emotions and personal interests, absorbing the time and attention of the other person. Taking is done in listening when one receives useful information, advice, or praise.

A productive discussion should contain a balance of give and take.

Developing Listening Skills

With all the listening opportunities there are in a lifetime, it seems too bad that the enjoyment and art of listening is so badly neglected. These listening games, suitable for family playing, may help to build listening power—one of the most important, and certainly the most neglected, of the language arts. In general, the games are listed beginning with the easy and moving to the more difficult.

Pack a Picnic

Begin by saying: "Today I am packing a picnic basket. I'll put in some pickles. What will you put in?" Each player repeats the articles already packed and adds his article. You may fill a toy box, Santa's pack, or a suitcase for a trip.

Surprise Sack

Each person chooses some object in the home and places it in a sack. Each takes a turn in describing his hidden surprise object without naming it. All listen attentively for the clues and try to guess what is in the sack.

Tall Tale

Someone in the family begins a story. When he stops, he chooses another to continue the story. Choosing another person, rather than taking turns, causes each person to listen more closely so he can "pick up" the story.

Don't Go Hungry

All listen while the person who is "IT" tells of his plans to go to the store. IT says, for example, "I will go to the store to buy some apricots, some beans, and some carrots"; all articles are named in alphabetical order. An adult holds up a card with one of the letters used, for example, *b.* The one who recalls the word "beans" first, gets to be IT. If he answers incorrectly, he must choose a new IT. The game moves on, the next person using the next letter.

Test Your Listening

Have someone read a short paragraph aloud and then ask questions about the content. Spice up the game with a humorous paragraph or a question which is not answered in the material. Do not prolong the game to the tiring point.

Word Families

Four words, three of which belong to the same classification, are given. Ask which are the three that belong together? For example: apple, grass, peach, orange. Five or more words may be used if the children are ready for that many.

Teakettle

Someone tells a short story in which he uses a pair or set of homonyms such as *to, two, too,* except that in the place of the homonym he says, "Teakettle." For example: Susan went *teakettle* the store. She bought *teakettle* apples. When she came *teakettle* the candy counter, she bought some of that *teakettle.* The player who states and spells the correct set of homonyms is the next leader. For alert players, two pairs of homonyms may be used in the same story.

What Did I Draw?

A person gives directions, such as, "Start near the top of your paper. With your pencil draw a line to the right for about two inches. Now go down about one inch, over to the right two inches, down one inch, to the right two inches, down one inch, and to the right two. What have you drawn?" (Stairsteps, I hope.) Directions for other simple figures, such as squares, rectangles, triangles, or buildings can be given. You may establish an approximate

"length" at the beginning and use it as a standard, whether inches or just a "length."

Where Are You Going?

One person begins by saying, "I am going to Chicago to buy a *c*ar. I am going to take along a *c*ane." Another person responds using two key words beginning with *c* and spelling them. For example, "I want to buy some *c*andy, c-a-n-d-y. I am going to take along a *c*arrot, c-a-r-r-o-t. That person then chooses another place beginning with another letter, such as, "I am going to *S*an Francisco to buy some *s*ugar. I am going to take along some *s*andwiches." Someone else will use *s* words to respond. You may test listening power even further by asking at the end of the game what countries or cities were visited.

What Is a Tree?

Have each member think of a given object, such as a tree. Ask each one to describe what he "sees" when he hears you say the chosen word.

Hot? Cold?

Think of words that may be used to describe degrees between hot and cold.

What Is He Like?

Prepare the following written description for each participant, substituting on *one* paper the word *warm* for the word *cold,* unknown to anyone else in the group: intelligent—skillful—industrious—cold—determined—practical—cautious. Pass out the papers and give these instructions:

"Here is a list of characteristics that belong to a particular person. Read them carefully and try to form an impression of the kind of person described. Then select from the following list those traits which are most in accordance with the picture of the individual you have

formed. Underline one in each pair."

1. Generous—stingy
2. Shrewd—wise
3. Unhappy—happy
4. Irritable—good-natured
5. Humorous—humorless
6. Sociable—unsociable
7. Popular—unpopular
8. Unreliable—reliable
9. Important—insignificant
10. Ruthless—humane
11. Good-looking—unattractive
12. Persistent—unstable
13. Frivolous—serious
14. Restrained—talkative
15. Self-centered—altruistic
16. Imaginative—hard-headed
17. Strong—weak
18. Dishonest—honest

Compare notes among the group.

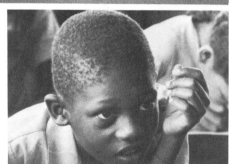

ACTING
a LiTTLe BiT OF MAGiC

Two girls start vigorously twirling the "rope." A boy steps between the girls and begins to jump. Up and up again he goes with strong, rhythmic beats. Twenty jumps. The arms of the girls swing evenly, and he doesn't miss a jump.

There is no music. There is no rope for this is a feat of imagination, a creative art without the use of "things" or props.

When God created man and woman, he created them in his own image, not only giving us heads but also bodies. Though we unconsciously reveal a great deal through our bodies, much of the time we hide behind our mind and words. We are much more inhibited in expressing ourselves with our bodies, even though nonverbal action tends to free the mind and emotions far more than words.

A person, by his very nature, lives in two worlds—the world of thoughts, dreams, and images and the physical world, both natural and man-made. In a child's world fantasy and reality are closely related. But the wonderful imagination with which children are endowed dies out or becomes dormant unless it is exercised. Like the muscles, it must have exercise if a person is to become a creative thinker.

The use of the imagination to create illusions is the key in creative drama. The expression is of the *whole* self in relationship to other persons and ideas. The idea may come from a word, a verse, a story, or an experience. It may come from literature, from life, or from "imaginings."

Playmaking, a term used interchangeably with creative dramatics, is play-living in which a child "tries on life" by putting himself in the place of any person who catches his interest, as well as all the animals, imaginary playmates, and inanimate objects he will likely "become" when he is about four. The child is exploring how it feels to be a strong truckdriver, a galloping horse, invisible Susie, a bouncing ball.

Dramatic play also provides an outlet for expressing emotions and relieving tensions. Life, to most people, is very dull without play. It is in search of a thrill that cars are stolen, fires are set, and houses entered. When a person cannot have excitement in real life, he seeks to experience it vicariously—in movies, TV, or sports. However, what is needed and is far more satisfying is active participation in which he can express his own feelings and ideas.

Creative drama develops initiative, resulting from thinking and expressing one's self independently. Resourcefulness is encouraged through considering and evaluating the various forms of expression. Freedom in bodily expression comes from exercise in expressing ideas through pantomime. Acting contributes toward a philosophy of living as the actor "lives" the life of many people. As he identifies with the characters, he examines their motives, relationships, attitudes, and ways of communicating. In doing so he wonders about his own way of living. Parents who are aware and put their imaginations to work on everyday problems will find innumerable ways of enriching family life through playmaking.

SoMe WaRM-UPs

Pretend you are doing something:

Brushing teeth, building a fire, pitching a ball, lifting a heavy object, walking through tall corn, wading in deep water, skating on ice, opening a surprise package, peeling a banana, blowing up a balloon, flying a kite.

Pretend you are being something:

A cat drinking milk, a dog scratching fleas, a bird taking a bath, a chicken drinking water, an animal you like best of all, a toy that makes you the happiest.

Lamb," "Jack Sprat," "Jack and Jill," "Boy Blue." Introduce conflict with "Tom, Tom, the Piper's Son"; "Pussy Cat, Pussy Cat"; "The Queen of Hearts"; "Three Men in a Tub."

Now, add dialogue:

Rhythm and repetition charm a small child—"Then I'll huff and I'll puff and I'll blow your house in" ("Three Little Pigs"); "Who's that tripping over my bridge?" ("Three Billy Goats Gruff") and "Who's been eating my porridge?" ("Three Little Bears").

Read a story and then dramatize:

"Cinderella," "The Little Red Hen," "Snow White," "Rumpelstiltskin," "The Elves and the Shoemaker," "The Emperor's New Clothes," "Mr. and Mrs. Vinegar."

Books for older children to act out:

Story of Ferdinand by Munro Leaf, *The Green Ginger Jar* by Clara Judson, *Tree of Freedom* by Rebecca Caudill.

Bible stories:

Parables: The Sower, The Talents, The Lost Coin, The Lost Sheep.

The children will understand these incidents: (1) when David refused the chance to take revenge on Saul (1 Samuel 26:1-12); (2) the quarrel between

pirate. Stretch it behind your back; you're a butterfly. Fling it high above your head and run lightly; you're a cloud. Tie it around your neck; you're a cowboy. Lay it out flat; it covers your doll.

Role playing:

When arguments or problems arise in the family or in the neighborhood, it is often difficult to get to the bottom of the trouble. "Let's play it out" may help to settle the controversy. Make up your own situations in which decisions need to be made. Act out the various solutions and evaluate. It is easier to see the dilemma when "You're someone else."

For parents who can "unbend" a little, these games are delightful for a family to play together. A stack of cards can be developed with ideas printed on them. Each in turn would draw a card. Avoid telling anyone what to do or how to do it. Don't expect perfection. The emphasis is on participation not the product.

IT'S A LITTLE BIT OF MAGIC

You will remember that Mary Poppins was magic. She had such an imagination that she caused suitcases and sidewalks to take on new wonder for children. With Mary Poppins, even taking medicine became strangely special, for

Act out words:

Hot, cold, good, funny, old, bumpy, dangerous, absent-minded, dreamy, sad, disgusted, disappointed, angry, happy.

Use nursery rhymes:

"Little Miss Muffet," "Mary Had a Little

Abraham and Lot over land (Genesis 13:1-12); or (3) the frantic anxiety of Zaccheus when the crowd refused to let him through to see Jesus (Luke 19:1-10).

Add a prop:

Tie a scarf around your waist; you're a

whenever she poured a spoonful of medicine she poured a spoonful of suggestions.

Perhaps you, too, can find a way of accomplishing something significant with the littlest bit of magic—imaginative and creative playmaking!

13

A Humdrummer for a Humdrum Day

Another day!

The Lord made it and you.

However you feel – it's yours.

Noiselessly the hourglass reminds us that time can slip through our fingers.

For everything there is a season, and a time for every matter under heaven. . . ." A day to bounce out of bed and sing, "Oh, what a beautiful morning," or a day to pull the covers up over your head and groan, "Oh, no, not *another* day!" Regardless of how you feel, another twenty-four hours are yours.

A commentator on the radio used to punctuate each news event with the declaration: "Time marches on!" Indeed it does. And most of us are keenly aware of its passing.

A grandfather clock divides and announces the hour with majesty and dignity.

tick tock

The staccato of the alarm clock calls us to duty. Its tick, tick, tick and nerve-shattering ring jolt our senses into reality and action. That marker of time says, "Up and at it," as it announces there's a new day dawning.

Perhaps the nervous tick of our watch regulates our lives even more demandingly. It's our constant companion, our reminder through the day that it's time to take the children, bake the pie, get the cleaning, catch the plane, shovel the snow, hear the report. Though handy, it will regiment our lives completely if we let it.

So an hour's an hour — sixty minutes, always the same. Or, is it? A four-year-old anticipating his birthday asks, "It is today, Mommie? Is it today?"

"No, not today. Just two more days." Just two more days! They will seem like an eternity to him; but to his mother there will not be time enough with clothes to wash, house to clean, favors to make, cake to bake.

Being fifteen-going-on-sixteen has its own feeling about time. In moments of breathtaking ecstasy a teen-ager would stop the hands of the clock. But stickers plastered on car windows, notebooks, walls, and jackets complain that too much time has already passed. They demand "Peace NOW!"

To one intensely involved in an activity, time seems to pass unnoticed. To one who is bored "time crawls through this desert of uneventfulness as though lame in both feet." He watches the clock incessantly, eager for release.

The days are ours to use, with some "givens," but we exercise our possibilities as human beings to the extent we decide to choose our attitudes toward each day. It is our decisions, moment by moment, that determine whether or not we glorify God in our lives.

Something to make time pass

Have you made a whistle from a willow sapling or from a wide blade of grass stretched tautly between your thumbs? Ever hummed a tune through tissue paper on a comb? Or, why not make a humdrummer for a humdrum day?

Some people, when they are afraid, whistle a tune to give themselves courage as well as to hide their fear. You can do the same thing whenever you feel sad or afraid." If you can't produce your own happy sound because you feel angry or anxious, gloomy or guilty, why not improvise a whistle?

Using all but the very last bit of waxed paper on the roll, I was left holding an interesting cardboard tube too good to toss away. I must have needed a whistle that day, for I immediately thought of the laughs we enjoyed with a humdrummer we used to make. It's a simple, silly little thing, but I thought someone in your family might have fun with it, too.

The tube can be found in many places — inside paper towels, aluminum foil, plastic film, tissue paper, waxed paper. It should be at least ten inches long, but not more than sixteen inches, and about one and one half to

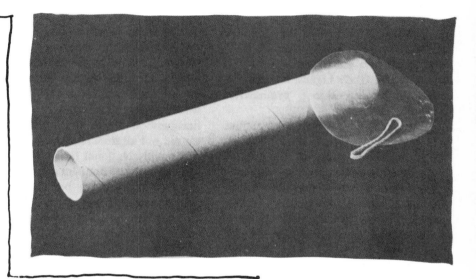

two and one half inches in diameter. Place a circle of waxed paper, larger than the tube, over one end. Secure it with a rubber band. It looks a bit like a drum; that's where it gets part of its name. With mouth slightly open, forming an "oo," hum your tune through the open end. As you hum, the waxed paper vibrates, creating an intriguing dimension to your melody.

If you want to be fancy, punch two or three holes about half an inch in diameter, beginning about one and a half inches from the covered end. Can you notice a change of tone as you play it like a flute or a piccolo?

One humdrummer makes a solo, two a duet, and three or more a humdinger of a humdrummer chorus.

RUBBINGS REVIVED

Touch, explore, twist, bend—or try a rubbing!

A young child has a special ability to respond openly to the world about him. Something catches his eye and he stops to look, touch, pat, poke, pick up, taste. His looking, his selecting, his trying out, his enjoying are part of his discovery and play. He is busy combining his own experiences with qualities which he sees in his environment. All these things have the potential to be useful or pleasurable in terms of his own individual sensory responses.

Some of this free, open exploring may become stifled with "Go straight to the store and come straight home" or by its very "usualness." Because he can see it everyday he may never really see it at all. But being truly alive is responding to the stuff around us — the sounds, the sights, the smells, the tastes, and the feel.

Characteristics of the kinds of things which affect their potental as materials we can use become the sensory element — can you see it, hear it, pick it up, touch it, handle it, smell it, move it? — and its workability — can you twist, turn, bend, cut, color, mark, tear, or fasten it?

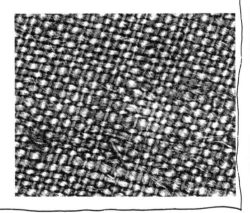

Within the broad range of tactile possibilities literally at our fingertips, we can select a smaller group for the patterns in making a rubbing, sometimes called *frottage*.

There is a special delight in running across something, in an unlikely place, which stimulates your imagination. You may pick it up because "it was just lying there until I came along" or "I saw some possibilities in this thing." You may idly pick it up — turning, twisting, observing it — and then begin to look for something else which will go with it, interact with it, help it.

But the stimulation and faith in one's own potential to discover and to explore such "finds" do not develop automatically. They grow out of imagination, initiative, adventure, pleasure, confidence, success, and even failure. We need to discover the appreciation for, the satisfaction of, and the response to the potentials which lie dormant *around* us and *in* us!

No doubt we were once told that good boys and girls "do not touch." Learning by running our hands over the surface of things has been gradually put aside until we have have almost forgotten the tactile qualities of wood grain, raw linen, mellow earth, or chips of brick in our now-world of globs and gobs of plastic. However, there is still a great variety of rough, bumpy, fluted, veined, scarred, sinewy surfaces to be discovered and enjoyed by our hands if we look around for them. Feel dramatically different textures — hair, a scrub brush, corduroy, silk, the carpet, the floor.

Most of us have pressed a sheet of paper over a penny, capturing Abe Lincoln with our pencil strokes. The same effect may be achieved by using the side of unwrapped wax crayons on sheets of fairly thin, soft paper (tissue, onionskin, or cheap newsprint). Try out the surfaces in your room — the floor, grilles, wooden bowls, cut glass, etched crystal, furniture patterns, tops of tin cans, book covers — whatever looks and feels likely. Then move on out the door, to the yard, the street, wherever your hunt leads you. The exploration will be longer and more enjoyable if several fellow hunters join you as companions in the search.

The longer you work at it the more skillful you will be at holding the paper stretched on the surface and at rubbing the crayon to capture the particular feel which interests you. If the paper slips and you get a double image, it may suggest the possibilities of repetition. Try making some parts appear very clearly and letting other parts fade out.

What you are looking for is something *you* like. Your own mixture of reasons for why you like it, based on your own experiences, is your guide. However, if you can *feel* the long, sweeping lines of the grain in a wooden plank, the clean, swinging arches of a garbage can lid, the irregular blockiness of a lizard handbag, or the intricate veining of a leaf, you will be involved in a creative experience rather than simply "making rubbings."

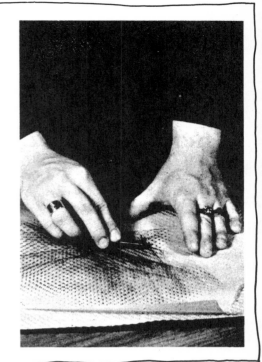

"**R**ubbing" is an ancient art which has been revived. Recently a museum featured the beautiful rubbings of early American gravestones made by a sixth-grade class. In Florence we saw art students making mammoth rubbings of the famous "Gate of Paradise" of the baptistry in Piazza del Duomo. In surface patterns from "Our Door to the Street" a family included staircase treads, the bottom of Tommy's sneakers, the cement walk, the street numbers of their home, the leaves of the shrubs.

Wax crayons make possible a batik or "wax resist" variation in the process of composing your rubbings. This is done by sponging ink, thinned water color, or poster paint over the rubbed pattern of colored wax. If the water color wash is black or a dark color, it will produce a dramatic reversal of the former order of light-dark contrasts. For example, a yellow pattern, formerly quite faint against the white paper, will stand out like a neon light.

But you may be so fascinated and pleased by the rubbing which you get that, to the batik "artist" who exclaims, "Look at this!" you will answer just as excitedly, "Wait till you see what I'm getting!"

A MATTER of CIRCLES

Translate a carpet of flowers—with chalk, tissue paper, and lots of color!

At La Orotava, Tenerife, in the Canary Islands we enjoyed seeing spectacular Carpets of Flowers designed to celebrate the religious holiday, Octave of Corpus Christi. For four blocks on each of three main streets these colorful carpets stretched continuously. Flower petals of brilliant hues, carefully arranged on the cobblestones, formed religious symbols, pictures, and designs in unbelievable detail. The sight was dazzling in its beauty and sobering in its reverence.

I recalled reading about the Chalk Carpet of Color Contest held in New York City in the fall of 1969. Hundreds of New Yorkers rushed to Central Park on the designated Sunday morning. Each was given a kit of various colored chalks and then was assigned a square yard of sidewalk as his "canvas" on which to paint. The contest was open to any individual over the age of fifteen years. The "artists" were given a free hand in expressing themselves as long as the designs were of a mosaic, geometrical, floral, or oriental pattern. For four hours they painted. The result was a vast carpet of color in Central Park.

No doubt, some drew mandalas for it is said that all over the world children draw mandalas. Basically, the mandala is a circle or a roundish shape of any kind. It is divided by two crossed lines, looking like a pie that has been cut into four equal pieces. Mandala means "circle" or "magic circle" in Sanskrit.

The basic idea has been used in religious art and in sand paintings of the Pueblo and Navajo Indians. Children and adults have been drawing them since primitive man picked up a sharp rock and scratched a drawing on the wall of his cave home.

Our wide driveways and smooth sidewalks are ideal places for drawing mandalas. Have available chalk of many colors. Yellow stars, blue triangles, pink flowers, swirls of all colors, and lots of squiggly lines will soon fill the mandalas. To cover an area thickly, crumbled colors may be rubbed into the pavement with the palms of the hand.

John Arms in the *Christian Science Monitor* says, "Just why mandala drawing comes naturally to children all over the world, nobody knows for certain. Some say the mandala is the child's version of the human face, which is the most important thing, in a young mind, about people. The criss-cross lines, say these experts, might represent the vertical line of the nose and the horizontal line of the eyes."

But probably when a child picks up a piece of chalk or a crayon, he simply wants to make a boundary for his drawing so he draws a circle. To break it up into smaller areas, he draws two lines. From there his imagination takes over, with long sweeping lines, concentrated little circles, and many unidentifiable shapes.

What a fun way to spend a warm spring day! Why don't you stage a Mandala Day in your community?

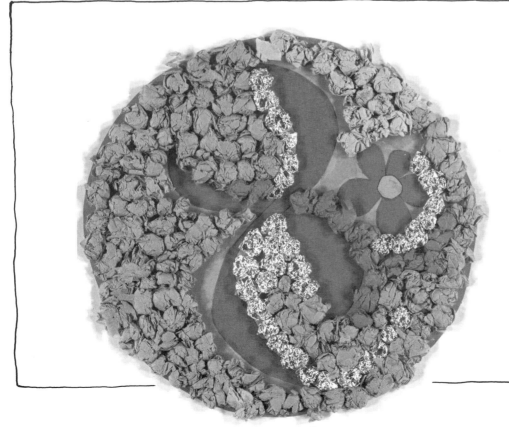

If it's a rainy day? Here's another kind of "carpet" or mandala — made of paper wads, of all things!

Draw a preliminary pencil sketch for the design. Later enlarge the design on various colors, sizes, and shapes of cardboard. Tear numerous colors of tissue paper into small pieces and crush them into small or large wads. Dip each wad carefully into paste and press it into place on the background surface. Apply these colored paper wads along the outline of your sketch, then fill in the solid areas within the design. You may cover either a portion of the cardboard or the entire area.

This produces an interesting carpet-like relief texture which looks a bit like the colorful Carpet of Flowers made by our Spanish friends in Tenerife.

MAKING SOME UNUSUAL SLIDES

As an amateur photographer have you made some "goofs" when a flash bulb failed to go off, the light wasn't bright enough, you moved, or someone else moved? Dig out those unshowables" and have fun with your mistakes.

USING A BLANK FILM

One idea for using these cast-off slides came from an article about Pablo Picasso. While photographing the sculpture of Picasso, the famous photographer Gjon Mili uncovered a completely unexpected facet of the artist's creative touch — miniatures.

The technique is to use a pin or sharp pocket knife to pierce or scratch a design on the dark film. The area within which you work is very small so keep the design simple — a few pin holes forming an outline and/or a minimum of short, sweeping lines giving the feeling of motion.

If some color or a partial picture is visible, use your imagination and capitalize upon it. This will add a touch of mystery in the composition of your design and will bring out the genius in you.

For variety words can be scratched on the black film. Felt markers can provide contrasting color. A lighted match held beneath the film will produce a psychedelic effect.

After the design is completed on the film, place it in the projector and throw the image on a screen. It literally "comes to life." Children and adults will be equally charmed by this experiment.

MAKE A SUBSTITUTE SLIDE

Take the film out of the slide and make a slide from magazine pictures. Beginning at the top of the frame, use a sharp knife to separate the back from the front. Remove the film. Select from magazines or catalogs colored pictures, words, or designs printed on shiny paper. Cut the selected material a bit larger than the film.

Carefully press transparent tape over the picture or design you have selected. Place it in the empty frame and glue the frame back together. For this simple process keep in mind that the print on the back of the picture will show through when the slide is projected on a screen.

MAKE A TRANSPARENCY

Use contact paper — the clear, plastic, self-adhering shelf paper — to make a transparency. Remove the film (see above). Cut a square of contact paper a little smaller than the frame. Peel the back off and mount the paper on the series of words or pictures desired. Using a hard object, rub out all the air separating the contact paper from the picture. Drop the square into a glass of clear tap water. In a few minutes remove the picture and the contact paper from the water. The paper will rub off the back of the plastic very easily. The clear plastic now holds your design or picture.

Lightly rub the excess pulp from the sticky side. Do this carefully. When the transparency is dry, mount it in the frame.

These slides are not as fine in quality as a regular slide, but I think you will find your imagination running wild with creativity as you work with this medium. Dennis Benson, who showed me this technique, says you learn by doing more. Do. Do. Do. He "blows a person's mind" by flashing pictures rapidly through the use of several projectors. He gets you involved! Make these slides for fun or for a teaching-learning situation.

CREATE A TRANSPARENCY

Remove the film and cut the contact paper as described above. Peel off the back of the contact paper and mount the transparent plastic in the frame. With a fine-line felt marker sketch your own outline, words, or design on the sticky side. When this artwork is projected you will be delighted with the enlarged, three-dimensional effect.

ADD A NEW DIMENSION

The real joy in looking at slides is the recalling of feelings associated with the experience. You are quickly transported back to the time when. . . . Choose a few family favorites. Select and play records which seem to express the mood or emotion felt in that setting. It may become interesting when members of your family discover that they did not share the same feelings at that time. Perhaps Sally was carsick the day Billy climbed up the mountain and *saw* the waterfall pictured in the slide. Can you find records which express the varied feelings of the family?

TISSUES— NOT FOR BLOWING BUT FOR DIPPING

You can make your own banners and gift wrap — with tissue paper!

THiS iS FoR EVeRYoNE...

It's simply amazing," wrote my mother, "that, whatever subject is studied, how much more there is to know!" This is the response I would expect from her as she listened to an enthusiastic glass collector tell the history of some unusual vases. She believes that learning is a lifetime process. It can take place anytime, at any age, without any special place or plan. Learning is a part of life, and life is a part of learning. What creates this aliveness? Ross Snyder in his book *On Becoming Human* observes, "The primary answer is to be caring — sensitively engaged in what's happening. Not cautious about life, but interested in nurturing life."

Walking with grandchildren looking for jack-in-the-pulpits, roasting weiners with youth who had helped to clear the brush from their timberland, lifting a tiny tot to see the wren's nest in a bucket hung over a fence post — these are the surprises and joys my parents share. Rachel Carson must have been thinking of folks like them when she wrote, "If a child is to keep alive his inborn sense of wonder . . . he needs the companionship of at least one adult who can share it, rediscovering with him the joy, excitement, and mystery of the world we live in." The generation gap is not felt by these seventy-five-plus-year-olds; for their experience is that when people laugh, work, and play together, they cease to be young and old. They become a group of persons simply enjoying their time together. Losing one's zest for life is the great sin of maturity.

How to keep young while getting older? Keep alive that curiosity and the thrill of discovery. Clay Bedford once said, "You can teach a student a lesson for a day, but if you can teach him to learn by creating curiosity, he will continue the learning process *as long as he lives.*" The glass buff who caught my mother's interest opened up a whole new area for her to explore. No vase will ever look the same to her again.

"At my age?" you ask. Yes, at your age — whatever it may be! Break out of the routine. Kick the habit of thinking "I'm too old." Do some fun things just for the sheer fun of doing them. What you didn't have time to do earlier in your life, explore now! *Take It From Here* is designed for young and old alike. It is for everyone. Come — join in the fun!

Looking over items in an import shop, I saw some delicately patterned Japanese wrapping paper. It was much too expensive for me to buy. But, why couldn't I make some of my own? In the library I learned that the Japanese had probably used rice or mulberry paper. What could I use instead? An art book suggested common two- or three-ply facial tissues. I tried it and it worked!

Since FOLD AND DIP is a bit messy, we're suggesting it as a backyard activity although, if you are careful, you can do it in the kitchen. You need:

- Common facial tissues (The large man-size is super)
- Coloring — dyes from any drug store
- Newspapers to cover your working area
- Shallow pans for the colors (Aluminum pie plates are fine)
- Paper towels on which to lay the color-dipped tissues

You prepare:

Colors are prepared in concentrated form. Dissolve a part of the contents of the packet of dye in a sauce pan of hot water. Strain through a fine mesh. (A nylon stocking works well.) The intensity of the color is lessened by the addition of water.

The simple process:

- Fold the facial tissue a number of times
- Dip in one or more colors
- Open it up carefully
- Place on a paper towel to dry

WHAT MaKES iT FUN?

The fascinating designs and patterns are dependent upon three factors:

- The many possible ways of folding the paper (triangles, rectangles, etc.)
- The ways of dipping the folded paper (edge, point, etc.)
- The length of time the folded paper is in the color (Since the tissue is very absorbent, the coloring process is brief.)

Do experiment! Facial tissues are cheap. This is where your creative and imaginative mind goes to work. Make several designs, varying the folds, the ways of dipping and the length of time the paper is left in the colors. Observe the characteristic designs which result. Experiment until you find one that suits *you*.

FiNiSHeD

When the papers are dry they should be ironed carefully. Pull apart the two or three layers of the tissues. The repeated design can be mounted in the form of a banner by putting a small amount of rubber cement on the slight overlap of one layer on another. Brush a bit of rubber cement on a thin stick or dowel pin and roll carefully onto one end of the tissue. This makes an attractive, silklike banner. Or, you can make lovely wrapping paper much like the expensive packet of Japanese rice paper I saw in the import store.

OR TRY FoLD aND BRUSH

The process is similar to Fold and Dip but allows opportunity to work on more controlled designs. The materials are the same except for the addition of a shallow pan of water and one or two soft brushes of different sizes.

This time the paper is folded simply and not too many times. It is then completely wet in the shallow pan of water and blotted thoroughly between paper towels to remove excess moisture. A design suitable as one unit of a repeat pattern is brushed on one side of the damp paper with a generous amount of coloring. The paper is then turned over and if the coloring has not completely penetrated, the design is repeated on this side. The remainder of the process is the same as with Fold and Dip. Beautiful designs can be achieved by partly dipping and partly brushing on the colors and so combining both the techniques.

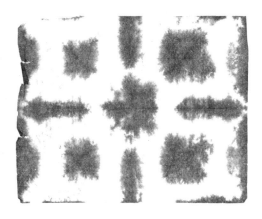

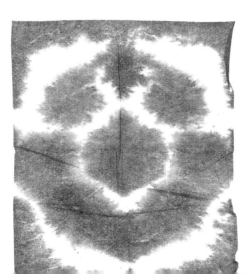

Fly with a Banner

On the tv program *Directions,* a teen-ager struggled to express her idea of the Jesus way of life. "It's . . . it's . . . it's loving someone you'd just love to hate." A ripple of laughter, then a hush fell over the group. The silence was broken by an explosive "Wow! Loving someone you would just *love* to *hate?* But . . . that's it. Yes sir, that's it!"

I was reminded of Clarence Jordan's remarks in *Sermon on the Mount:* "Jesus didn't tell his followers to love their enemies because love would or would not work. The idea probably never occurred to him to raise the question of whether or not it was practical. . . . Being what he is, God can't help loving all men, regardless of what they are. Even so with God's sons. Their nature is not determined by the reaction of their enemies, since by virtue of their complete surrender to the divine will they no longer have the freedom to cease being what they are. Bound by this higher loyalty, the argument of practicality is irrelevant to them. They do not for the sake of convenience set aside their nature, any more than a minnow transforms into a bird when in danger of being swallowed by a bass."

Now... let your imagination fly!

Clarence Jordan used his imagination. Why don't you? Away you go! Free and on your own! How about a banner or poster to brighten up some room on a dreary, wintry day? Once you decide on such a project, idea after idea will begin to pop into your mind. Some slogans? Look all around you. Listen carefully. In *Sound of Music* I heard, "Love is not love 'til you give it away." On a church bulletin board I saw, "All my tomorrows depend on your love." In the Bible I read, "Make love your aim" and "Love never ends" and "Love one another" and "God is love."

If making letters is not your cup of tea, unique color combinations, unusual letter shapes, and an unconventional arrangement of just the simple word — love, peace, hope, *pax,* or *shalom* — make eye-catching banners or posters. Or, use symbols, such as the dove, which suggest words or meanings.

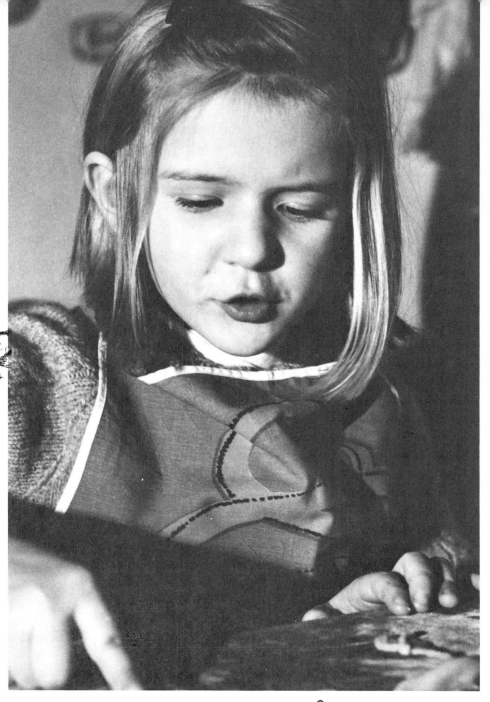

Kids, surprise your family; make and share with them your very own creation. Mom, perk up a "blah" wall with a brightly colored burlap banner — fringe and all. Or, wouldn't it make an exciting family project, accompanied by bowls of crunchy popcorn and some sweet, juicy apples?

Burlap or felt provide the best background for banners. Designs or letters made from yarn, bits of felt, rick-rack, or buttons may be pasted or sewed on the material. A dowel pin across the top makes for an easy and attractive hanging. Fringe, tassels, braids, yarns, or various other trimmings added to the bottom make a festive banner.

Construction paper, bright crayons, poster paint, chalk, or pastels, yarn, string, and bright odds and ends of paper may be used for a poster.

Keep the design simple but full of action and color. Letters need not all be the same size or shape, you know. Maybe a good photograph has caught your eye or a picture of your family is something special to center the poster around.

Do your thing! It's *the* thing! Banners and posters are the *in* thing!

Try a poster... or, choose brightly colored cloth for a festive banner

25

Phil is a minister-friend who takes everyday experiences and turns them into a kind of homespun philosophy of life and living. He shares his mental wanderings with his parishioners in a weekly column, "Pastor's Pulse." Humorous events may trigger serious contemplation; a bit of wit may break through a time of trouble.

Dogs, skunks, chickens, horses, or children furnish material for Phil as do shopping centers, drive-ins, TV commercials, and accidents. Human frailties, foibles, frivolities, and frustrations provide the touch which makes the column so intriguing. Phil writes in his own inimitable style:

"This past week I listened as a trio of teen-agers shared the excitement they had attempting to catch a skunk. They knew, of course, that they were flirting with potential disaster, but still they proceeded to follow their plan.

"They noticed that the skunk had hidden under the porch, so they decided to catch him at a narrow entrance as he left. One boy stood on the porch with a forked stick raised over the narrow opening and was prepared to push the stick over the skunk's head as he emerged.

"After all plans had been made, the other boys started throwing rocks and tin cans at the porch. Sure enough, the skunk came out and the stick came down. Immediately the air was filled with a new odor, but the only damage was under the porch. Next, two brave souls proceeded to pull the skunk the rest of the way through the small opening while the other hero was going to grab the skunk's tail and hold it high before he could do any more damage.

"But he missed! And before anyone could holler, 'Right Guard,' all three boys were polluted and the rest of their evening was shot.

"One remarked to me in recalling the incident, 'You can bet I'll never try that again!' And I'll bet he won't either. I only wish that sin would work the same way. If only the air or our clothing would be filled with a very pungent odor whenever we sinned then perhaps it wouldn't be so hard to stop. But sin doesn't stink—or does it?"

Life is no ho-hum, humdrum, boring existence for Phil! He takes the ordinary and makes of it the out-of-the-ordinary. He's a bit like the artist Graham Sutherland, who remarked that he never walked into his garden each morning without expecting to see something he had never seen there before. Perhaps because we can see "it" every day, we may never really see it at all.

Look beyond the ordinary

A camera can help you pause in your rush through life to see beyond the ordinary in the common events of the day. Photography can be an extra sense or a reservoir for the senses. As you focus through the view finder, you will see a person, an object, a scene, an action in a new and different way.

Edwin Land was quoted in *Time* as saying:

"I find each new person whom I meet a complete restatement of what life and the world are all about. The individualization of people—individualization of spirit, taste, emotion—this is what makes life ageless. . . . Photography can teach people to look, to feel, to remember in a way that they didn't know they could."

When you take a picture you cannot get into it all the feelings you have at that particular time, but you can capture enough so that when you look at the picture it will bring back most of the memories associated with it.

Seeing Things in a NEW Way

Look down, look up, look all around

Experiment with your camera! Nobody's pictures are all good. Even the most practiced professional turns out some poor pictures. He just doesn't show them to anyone. Often a good picture is pure luck. Sometimes it's the inborn ability of the photographer to recognize a promising picture situation. Most of the time, however, it is the skill acquired through experience. Since black-and-white film is the cheapest, why not experiment in *chiaroscuro,* a study in which only light and shade produce the effect of a third dimension? It would be a fun beginning!

Some simple tips

1. Don't always take "see the birdie" pictures—those posed ones which must be explained with, "Oh yes, this is of Johnny on Mother's Day a year ago when he fell in the lake while fishing." Wouldn't you rather see one of him actually involved in the fateful fishing mission? Photos of children most likely to become treasures are those in which the kids are busily engaged in just being themselves.

2. Adults are difficult to photograph because they quickly snap to the position of "Attention!" Shoot your picture when your subject is so engrossed in some personal activity that he won't notice your photographic pursuits. What people do is often as interesting photographically as what they look like.

3. Framing a picture tends to separate the subject from his surroundings and helps the viewer to concentrate on the subject. It contributes to a feeling of unity. If the framing devices—trees, fences, windows, and bridges—are much nearer the camera than the subject, they also communicate a feeling of depth.

4. Pictures should always be made from as close as possible without eliminating any part of the subject that's important to the snapshot or any part of the background that contributes to the meaning or the mood of the picture.

5. Horizontal lines communicate rest— a man stretched out asleep on his back. Diagonal lines connote action—an athlete straining forward.

6. Remember that your camera looks beyond the subject—and so should you. A detailed, distracting, "busy" background will make a picture look sloppy and cluttered and will detract from the subject. The best snapshot backgrounds are generally plain ones.

7. Deliberate distortion can play an important part in adding drama or humor to a picture.

Get to the bottom of things

Don't limit yourself to only one approach. Start with a long shot and then come in close. Shoot against light. Pick out details and record them. Look down and around; look up and under. See things from an unusual perspective. You will find that a single subject can provide for a whole afternoon of interesting shooting if you take the ordinary and make an extraordinary or an out-of-the-ordinary narrative—in picture form!

Carving
with color

If you saw an old man cutting up brightly colored paper, you might think he was piddling away his time in child's play. Yet colored paper and scissors in the hand of Henri Matisse produced great art. His colored paper cutouts, in their simplicity, seemed to sparkle and dance.

Matisse came upon colored cutouts almost by accident. Earlier he had used paper models in designing his paintings by moving them around on his canvas until they resulted in an arrangement which pleased his eye. In 1941, at the age of seventy-two, Matisse was confined to his bed with an illness which prevented his painting at an easel. Propped up in bed he began to make cutouts which became more than a simple substitute for painting for they were comparable in their vitality to his paintings.

"To cut right into color makes me think of a sculptor's carving into stone," he once wrote of his new art. Manipulating his scissors as he might a chisel, Matisse carved human figures, leaves, flowers, and fish into decorative compositions. Some of them were complete pictures; others were used as posters, magazine covers, church decorations in stained-glass windows, vestments, and other designs.

He placed the cutouts on white or multicolored backgrounds, moving them around as he had done on his easel. These "carvings" provided a fitting conclusion to his lifework as a master of design and color.

Paper is a versatile material. It is essential and practical in its utilitarian qualities; yet it is challenging to the imagination and essential as a medium of expression.

In many communities of the world, paper has played an important part in cultural life and in artistic enrichment.

The paper cutouts of Poland, known for their vibrance and expressiveness, have been recognized as a folk art. In Mexico paper has a prominent place in many festivals when banners, piñatas, and various other constructions provide elaborate spectacles.

Paper folding, *origami,* is a favorite pastime for both children and adults in Japan but is significant enough to be featured in art exhibits. The making of silhouettes was once an art sponsored in convents throughout Europe. Like Matisse, many painters have found paper useful for cutting shapes to be studied and related as they plan the composition of their pictures.

Cutouts

Your name will make an interesting design. Write or print your name in fairly large letters along the edge of a fold in a sheet of paper, using a crayon or broad-tipped felt pen. Cut along either side of the line with paper folded, being careful not to cut too close to the fold. Now unfold the paper. Aren't you surprised at the intricate and fascinating design?

Cut circles, triangles, or squares of all sizes and in all colors. Arrange on contrasting color of paper. Experiment with shapes of fruit or vegetables, the burst of fireworks, the ripple of water.

Torn paper

If cutting paper is "old hat" to you, try tearing it. Watch your mental images take visible shape as you tear, organize, and paste pieces of colored construction paper to create a picture you like.

Practice by tearing and shaping pieces of newspaper before you start working with construction paper. Tear slowly so you can think creatively as you tear and so you can feel the sensitive edges of the shapes as they unfold from your fingers.

After some experimenting, you are ready to try your skill with construction paper. Hold it between your fingers and slowly tear out a shape that you see in your mind. Because the irregular edge—controlled in places and accidental in others—gives a unique quality to the shape, you will not want to sketch outlines or use patterns as guides. Instead you will find it much more creative and exciting to draw upon your own ingenuity, feeling, and intuition. That is what creating with torn paper is all about.

After arranging the "torn creations" in your own special way, mount them on a sheet of harmonizing colored construction paper. Your theme may be realistic, decorative, or abstract. Color photographs and advertisements in magazines may be incorporated into the picture to add texture, variety, and contrast. Torn paper construction paved the way for collage.

Collage

In 1912, Picasso invented a new technique called "collage" by pasting on his canvas a piece of oil cloth printed to look like chair caning. With his sensitivity and his imagination, this great artist used very unusual materials and won for them an acceptable place in the art world.

The term collage is derived from the French *coller* meaning "to paste." Georges Braque followed Picasso's innovation and added newspaper into a still life canvas of fruit. Schwitters, Motherwell, and Burri have produced forceful pictures with torn paper and what is popularly known as "junk." Marca-Relli and Vincente are contemporaries primarily concerned with tearing and pasting materials on canvas.

Collage by its very nature is excellent for experimentation and discovery.

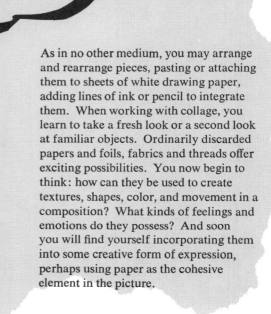

As in no other medium, you may arrange and rearrange pieces, pasting or attaching them to sheets of white drawing paper, adding lines of ink or pencil to integrate them. When working with collage, you learn to take a fresh look or a second look at familiar objects. Ordinarily discarded papers and foils, fabrics and threads offer exciting possibilities. You now begin to think: how can they be used to create textures, shapes, color, and movement in a composition? What kinds of feelings and emotions do they possess? And soon you will find yourself incorporating them into some creative form of expression, perhaps using paper as the cohesive element in the picture.

29

Treasures From Trash

"Sparrows don't drop candy wrappers," writes Margaret Gabel in her book by that title. "Beavers build no billboards. Trees don't shed tin cans. Dolphins don't dump chemicals into the water." Then why do we?

Pollution of the air, water, and land is a people problem! It is caused by our demand for faster transportation, for more convenience gadgets, for more things. Our motto seems to be "the bigger the better" or "the more we have, the happier we'll be."

Everything we buy is mechanized or sanitized. It either makes a noise, runs on wheels, grinds, chops or slices, or is fully automated. Our hamburgers and shakes are served with napkins, bags, wrappers, paper cups, lids, and drinking straws. Such a throwaway society produces a huge accumulation of trash. One year's trash from New York City would make a mile-high mountain in the middle of Yankee Stadium or fill a freight train seven miles long. The trash from Los Angeles would fill the Panama Canal in a year. As the earth becomes more crowded, there is no longer an "away" for our throwaways. One person's trash may be another's living space.

Trash is an American luxury. In Trinidad a lovely mahogany carving was simply handed to us with no wrapping to protect it. In Gran Canaria a tapestry was rolled up and tied with a string. In Italy a leather purchase was enclosed in a piece of paper just large enough to cover the article. In England housewives carried unwrapped fruit and vegetables in their mesh-like shopping bags. In Germany the loaves of bread were delivered "in the nude." In Norway a pewter tray was soon smudged with our fingerprints. And in Nigeria the brass deer's sharp antlers pricked our hands as we carried it.

With all the excess trash in the

United States, "out of sight, out of mind" seems to be the attitude of the litterbugs who casually drop anything and everything wherever they happen to be. Because they were disturbed about littering along the highways, one family drove twenty miles out of New York City and walked one-tenth of a mile picking up trash. They found 148 cans, 48 bottles, 137 pieces of paper, 30 pieces of auto parts and plastic containers. Scientists are searching for a container which will return to nature quickly, but it seems unlikely that anyone will come up with a container that is more successful than the ice cream cone!

What comes & goes in your home?

Two days in Rome while the garbage collectors were on strike made us keenly aware of the importance of the sanitation department, but as long as the garbage and trash cans are collected regularly from our doorsteps, few of us seem to care where all our refuse goes. Perhaps you will be in for a surprise if you keep a record of what comes in the door and goes out via the wastebasket in your home. You will see lots of things that—shouldn't have come into the house in the first place, might have been recycled by taking them back to the store to be used again, might have been things disabled veterans or the Salvation Army could use and might have collected, or things that could be mended or used in some creative and imaginative way.

Redemption art

Beautiful Junk: A Story of the Watts Towers by Jon Madian is the story of an angry boy in a dirty city, who first mocks a man as a back-alley junk collector, follows him, and discovers something of great importance to himself. The title suggests that many things which are thrown away can become "beautiful junk" or can be combined to make something pleasing to the eye.

John Grinnell Harrell, in *Teaching Is Communicating,* writes:

In almost every case where we have used creative or creativity, we might have used the word redemptive or redemption. For redemption may be thought of as the act of picking up the pieces, of establishing wholeness and identity. In creative expression we pick up the pieces of experience, give them unity and wholeness, and also an identity.

Perhaps junk art can be called "redemption" art.

Scrapwood art

"If Louise Nevelson can't find what she wants," exclaimed a fellow artist, "she scavenges the neighborhood for broken wheels, bowling pins, fruit crates, dowel pins, and other wooden bric-a-brac." These found objects lose their own special identity to form her famous giant, three-dimensional walls. One such wall, twenty-eight feet long and eight and one half feet high, is composed of one hundred fruit crates. Besides her walls of various shapes and sizes, Louise Nevelson makes pillars of these throwaway things. Her works are sprayed all black, all white, or all gold. The charm of her art is the shadows produced by the unusual objects and the way she uses them.

Are there odds and ends of wood around a new house near you? by a carpenter's shop? in your family's workshop? along the seashore? In Curaçao we found a delightful arrangement of bits of wood polished by the sea. René combined pieces of scrap wood with seed pods, which she found along the roadside, to make her wall hanging or mural. Shanna used all sizes and shapes of weathered wood for her modernistic figure. Why don't you try making something beautiful from scrap wood?

Junk art

Everywhere you look you will find bolts, screws, bottle caps, washers, rings from pull-top cans, parts of cars, or pieces of tools. Left out in the open, the materials take on a character of their own through bleaching, rusting, or bending. Collect some of this junk and make some form which is attractive to you. Turn the pieces around, fit them together in different ways, thread one through another. Use fine wire, twisting it tightly to hold the pieces in place. If it is a family project, the pieces might be soldered together. Picasso's famous *Bull's Head* has as its focal point a cast-off bicycle seat!

Today I visited that place where the garbage men dump their rubbish . . . how beautiful that was! Tomorrow they are sending me a few worthwhile objects collected from that heap—among others broken street lanterns to look at or to be used as model—if you wish. The whole thing was like an Andersen fairy tale. What a collection! All these old objects which have resigned their services— baskets, kettles, bowls, oil cans, metal wires, street lanterns, clay pipes. . . .

This exciting adventure to a rubbish dump was written by Vincent van Gogh to his friend Anthon van Rappard in 1883.

Try looking at junk through the eyes of van Gogh and see what you can make!

From Curaçao, wood washed from the sea makes a work of art

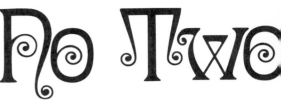

"If we could but read it, every human being carries his life in his face. . . . On our features the fine chisels of thought and emotion are eternally at work." Thus Alexander Smith reminds us that each one of us is a sculptor; our material is our own flesh and blood and bones. A countenance molded by amiable feelings acquires a beauty all its own because such feelings stamp their mark indelibly upon it. Pride, jealousy, envy, hatred, contempt, and fear etch their tell-tale lines upon the face. In the Shakespearean play, Hamlet says, "God has given you one face, and you make yourself another." Or, "a man of fifty is responsible for his face."

In the phrase "children's faces looking up, holding wonder like a cup" Sara Teasdale captured the imagery of innocence and awe. We envision the openness, the simplicity, and the trust so characteristic of a small child. The words, "when grace is joined with wrinkles it is adorable for there is an unspeakable dawn in happy old age," prompt us to recall the beauty in the faces of older persons we know and love. Daniel Webster once remarked, "In this sea of upturned faces there is something which excites me strangely." This stimulation, this excitement, this responsiveness in the faces of his audiences produced a great orator.

The sad, frightened face of a child who is lost gives way to one of radiance and relief when he sees his mother's face again. One cannot forget the exhilarating and delightful experience of seeing a familiar but unexpected face in a crowd of strangers. It is by the face that one person is known and distinguished from another, yet there are so few parts composing it and in a space so small.

The language of the face is understood by all peoples. The smile, an expression of friendship, is returned by those living in Africa. A look of bewilderment brings unsolicited help in locating a hotel in Norway. The puzzled expression when languages differ brings an interpreter in Caracas. As the language of the face is universal so is it very comprehensive. It is not only the index, but also the shorthand, of the mind. It crowds a great deal in a little room for a man may look a sentence while speaking a word.

The human face is the masterpiece of God. There is something in a face, an air, a peculiar grace which is most difficult for even the best of painters to capture. The wonder of it all is how among so many millions of faces there should be none that are alike!

Faces Alike

So it is with little "apple people." Everyone falls in love with Apple Grandma and Grandpa. They have an air of having grown old gracefully, wrinkles and all.

The largest solid apple you can find will be none too big for the head, for the apple will shrink a great deal in drying. Pare the apple and carve the features, being careful to have the nose protrude the farthest and making quite deep eye sockets. Make a few faint wrinkles with your fingernail. The rest of the wrinkles will take care of themselves.

Now hang it up to dry for about four or five weeks. If dried properly, it will last for years. When it is dry, color the cheeks and lips lightly with a bit of rouge. A light coat of shellac will preserve the features and enable bits of cotton, nylon hair, or yarn to be glued on. Use pins or beads or dried beans for the eyes. Rice may be inserted for teeth.

Fashion bodies from clothes hangers, bending into a framework with arms and legs. Design and make clothing for the miniature people. Grandma's dress may be made from a scrap of black satin or taffeta. Use a piece of old felt for her bonnet. Accessories, a ribbon, a touch of lace will give Grandma a sophisticated air.

Some of you may not see Grandma or Grandpa in the facial features or expression of your dried apple. You may see an old salt of the sea, a lass with a roving eye, some gossipy old busybodies. Dress your "applehead" to look like the person you see in the face. You may find that your apple people seem to come to life as you become acquainted with them.

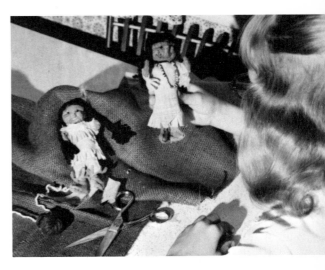

An African carving

Whittle Away Your Time

Carving is as old as civilization; it is as modern as tomorrow. We viewed with awe Michelangelo's *Pieta* in St. Peter's in Rome and his *David* in the Academy in Florence, but we also admired the free flowing lines of the white marble *Penguins* by Constantin Brancusi and the black granite form, *Construction out of Circular Ring* by Max Bill in the Art Institute, Chicago.

Carving is a "subtractive" art because the artist must remove, or take away, material. It is a sculptural art because it has three dimensions. Carved sculpture may be of three types: (1) in the round, where the figures may be seen from all sides; (2) relief, where the figure stands away from the background; and (3) intaglio, where the figure is cut below the background.

There is no best way to begin a carving. One sculptor will make a drawing; another may carve spontaneously with only a mental image of what he hopes to release from the materials. Regardless of the medium, before the project is started you will want to decide on the type of sculpture. Will it be realistic or abstract? What will be the size and proportion of the construction? If it is to be an animal, what action will the animal assume? If an abstract design is planned, what emotion or feeling do you want to convey? Will there be any suggestion of motion? Any connotation of symbolism?

Try wax, soap, or wood to start

Wax is a popular medium for a beginner. Ready-made candles offer a great range of artistic possibilities. The best are those that have color throughout. If the candle becomes soft from the heat of your hands, set it aside for a while. Fine lines, however, are more easily carved when the wax is soft. In carving remember that any material which is subtracted cannot be replaced. Think, visualize, and work cautiously, turning the sculpture around to view it from all angles. To achieve the antiqued effect, acrylic paint may be brushed on.

Wax is often thought of as an amateur's medium. But when visiting the Metropolitan Museum of Art, we saw *Woman Bathing* by Edgar Degas. Originally it was a small wax sculpture, discovered in perfect condition after the artist's death and cast into bronze by his heirs.

Soap has a tremendous potential for a carver of any age. Even failures don't go to waste for they can always be used for washing. For large figures join two bars of soap by cutting, with a wet knife, a thin layer from the sides to be joined. Hold the pieces tightly against each other until they are fused. A coat of clear plastic spray glaze will protect the surface of your finished product. Milda Morse has achieved some very sophisticated carvings in soap. Her *Seascape* includes several bars of different colors.

Wood carvings range from tiny whittled figures to huge forms carved from logs with a power saw. For a beginner, a piece of pine is the easiest to work. It cuts sharp and clean and is easy to carve with hand tools. Experience is the best way to learn about wood and what happens when you begin to carve it. Cutting with the grain is easier than cutting across the grain. Knots, burls, and the grain of the wood can be used to an advantage if you plan carefully.

Or, use simulated stone

Though carving in stone dates to prehistory, twentieth-century artists are rediscovering stone as a medium for artistic expression, simulating the simple forms of primitive art rather than the realistic forms.

A beginner will find man-made stone easy to carve. You will need a cardboard container in which to cast the stone— a shoe box, a round cereal box, a milk carton, or (if you are planning a relief or intaglio) a lid of a box or a pie tin. The shape and size of the container determines the character and dimension of the sculpture. Paring knives, sandpaper, and steel wool are all you will need for tools.

Recipes for Simulated Stone: The basic procedure for mixing and casting is the same for all recipes. Mix the dry ingredients in a bowl. Add enough water to produce a thick, pasty consistency that can be poured into the container. Shake the box well to eliminate air bubbles. Wash the mixing spoon and bowl immediately. Do not pour the residue down the drain. Colored ink, vegetable coloring, or dry or liquid tempera may be added.

Girostone is a combination of vermiculite (found at garden nurseries), cement, and sand. The proportions vary according to the hardness or softness desired. The more vermiculite, the softer the girostone and the easier to carve. For the softer girostone, about 4 parts of vermiculite are used to 1 part cement and 1 part sand.

Simulated stone may also be made from cement, sand, and Zonolite, an insulating material found at lumber yards. Use 1 part sand, 1 part cement, 3 parts Zonolite.

Plaster of Paris may be used for carving. Fill the pan with an amount of water equal to the desired amount of plaster. Sift plaster into the water, mixing it carefully by hand. As soon as the plaster begins to thicken, pour it into cardboard molds. A little salt will speed the thickening process; a little vinegar will slow it. A pinch of salt and a few drops of glycerin may be added to lessen chipping.

Carving the Stone: When the mixture is dry enough to carve (about three days for a cement mixture), tear off the paper container and begin to make your "chunk of stone" come alive, or as Michelangelo would say, "release the image that is already inherent within it."

To keep the mixture from drying out, wrap it in the plastic which comes from the cleaners. A quick immersing in water will restore the moisture content if the stone becomes too dry.

Try one form—or try them all! Which medium? Oh, try them all, too!

Puppets
Are Where You Find Them

"Dearly beloved brethren,
Do you think it is not a sin
To peel potatoes and throw away the skin?
The skins feed the pigs;
The pigs feed you.
Dearly beloved brethren,
Is not this true?"

With the simplest puppet on her hand, my older cousin delighted us younger ones with its antics. We sat entranced as she draped a large handkerchief over her thumb and two fingers, tucked the loose ends under the last two fingers, and held the ends in the palm of her hand. With head (index finger) bobbing up and down and arms (thumb and second finger) gesturing wildly for emphasis, the "preacher" came alive. We never grew tired of this "little old man" who expounded on the relationship of pigs, potatoes, and man long before ecology was a popular concern.

Although puppetry is an ancient art, it is not an old-fashioned one. Ask a child today what he knows about puppets, and he immediately identifies them with television. Puppets need not be complicated or expensive. All you need are such commonplace items as scissors, needle and thread, some everyday art supplies, and imagination. Imagination, of course, is the most important ingredient. A puppet not only can be made from practically anything but also can portray any thing—women, men, children, or animals—but it takes imagination to bring these puppets to life!

A scrap basket is a must. Odds and ends of jewelry, bits of yarn and wool, lace, pipe cleaners, feathers, fur—anything that can be glued, stapled, or stitched to another material. A good scrap basket can be the inspiration for ingenious creations. Wool yarn works beautifully for hair. Make it curly by wetting the wool strands and wrapping them around a pencil, secure, and let dry. Fur makes good hair, and steel scouring pads make fine curls. Cotton and steel wool serve as grayish hair. Curl or braid crepe paper for interesting effects. Frayed cloth, bits of cotton, cut wool strands, or fur make good beards.

Broom straws or string stiffened with glue are convincing whiskers. Eyelashes can be very glamorous when made with fringed and curled stiff paper. They can give a coy, a "wide-awake," or a sad look.

Circles cut from paper, buttons, or beans are only a few things which can substitute for eyes. Add wire, paper, cardboard, or pipe cleaner eyeglasses with cellophane added for the lens. Insect feelers or animals whiskers will wave back and forth in a realistic way if made from wire or pipe cleaners. Add brightly colored beads for a striking effect.

OUT OF A PAPER BAG?

Because it is so simple to make, the paper bag puppet is a good beginning project. By simply placing your fingers in the bottom of a flattened No. 2, 5, or 8 brown paper bag and moving the folded bottom up and down, you get the impression that your bag is "talking." The fold is the dividing line of the puppet's mouth. The upper lip is immediately above the fold, the lower part of the mouth immediately below. Once you get the relationship of the parts, all sorts of ideas for a puppet will pop into your mind.

Use paint, crayons, or felt-tipped pens to color and draw in the facial features. Paste on yarn for hair, buttons for eyes, ears cut from paper, and for an added flourish a fur mustache. For clothes, a paper tie and buttons down the front

of a skirt or a suit and "Ah-ha" your puppet has come alive!

A SISTER

Using a paper bag in another way, you can have a different kind of puppet. With the bag folded, cut away two V-shaped sections to make a neck. Unfold the bag. On the sides of the front section cut two armholes. Draw a face and costume. Add hair, if you like.

Tie a string or ribbon around the neck, leaving enough room to insert your three middle fingers into the head. Put your thumb and little finger into the armholes to make your puppet perform. Instead of a "talking" puppet, you have an "acting" puppet who can gesture with its arms (your fingers) and head.

TRY ONE IN CONSTRUCTION PAPER

Using an eight-by-twelve-inch sheet of construction paper, you can make another puppet in a jiffy. Place the twelve-inch side at the top and fold the paper into three equal parts. Fold the bottom up to meet the top. Now fold each of the two new top edges *down* to meet the center fold on the *outside*. You have the basic puppet shape. The two middle folds form the mouth. Slip your four fingers into the top open space and your thumb into the bottom one. Open and close your hand, and the puppet's mouth opens and closes, too. (Note Figures 1, 2, 3, and 4.)

A dog? A rabbit? A cowboy? Your puppet can take any form you wish. You can make your puppet larger by covering the basic form with larger pieces of colored paper. Decorate with collage materials, such as buttons, yarn, fur, or bits of colored paper. Features may be added with crayons, paints, or felt-tipped markers.

PAPER PLATE TO PUPPET

A paper plate offers a very sturdy surface for pasting and stapling. By folding the plate in half, the outer rim forms the lips of a wide mouth, and the fold furnishes the hinge which allows the mouth to open and close. Manipulate as in the construction paper puppet. Half of another paper plate stapled or glued to the forward edges of the upper part of the mouth, but free at the back, provides a pocket

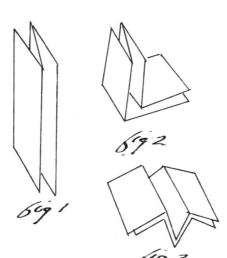
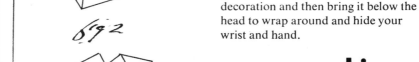

fig 1

fig 2

fig 3

4 fingers
thumb

fig 4

into which you can slide your fingers for better control.

Paper plate puppets can be made most imaginative by adding all kinds of fanciful decorations. You can drape a piece of cloth over the puppet's head as decoration and then bring it below the head to wrap around and hide your wrist and hand.

MOST ANYTHING GOES!

A simple cardboard cutout colored with crayons and taped to a ruler can make a captivating performer. I've seen tongue depressor puppets, wooden spoon puppets, stick puppets, and dowel pin puppets. These are rod puppets. You control them by the slim, rigid support. They can be moved around the stage, turned from side to side, moved up and down, and tilted in any direction. You will want a "stage" behind which to maneuver these characters. With some imagination and practice the stick or rod puppet can come alive, even though it is not nearly as manageable as other types.

Out-of-the-ordinary puppet-making material is everywhere—on the beach, in the attic, in the junk pile. Puppets are where you find them!

Note: You may want to use some of the puppets described here when you are using the activities suggested in the chapters on "Acting—A Little Bit of Magic" and "Stretching Your Imagination."

rotini, rigatoni, mostaccioli? Yes, macaroni! And toothpicks and clothes hangers and aluminum foil! They may not be the media you associate with sculpturing, but some modern artists have broken away from the age-old concept of sculpture as a "centralized totem" made of marble or stone. Sculpture of the twentieth century differs from the forms of classical Greece, the Renaissance, or the realism of the mid-1880s. Modern sculpture reaches out to involve the viewer. The design is one of openness. Space is emphasized as an important element in the design. The materials tend to be those that we use in our everyday living.

Some feel that today's sculpture reflects a "pleasing disregard for traditional sculptural procedures," while others feel this disregard has produced unaesthetic, even ugly, pieces which are undeserving of being called art. The controversy over Picasso's largest sculpture, *Construction, 1967,* in the Chicago Civic Center Plaza points up strikingly the differences in art appreciation.

Today's artists are intrigued with geometric construction—the mystery of numbers and proportion, equation and balance. "Why does a circle fascinate me?" wrote Vasily Kandinsky. The circle is "a single tension that carries countless tensions within it."

This fascination with the beauty of geometry has resulted in the construction of mobiles, stabiles, or the more conventional forms which speak of our technological age in either design or in media. The qualities in Constantin Brancusi's *Bird in Space* and Alexander Calder's *Lobster Trap and Fish Tail* in the Museum of Modern Art left much to our imagination and interpretation. This sculpture was in contrast to the realism graphically portrayed in the sculptural forms in the Gefion Fountain in Churchill Square, Copenhagen, Denmark, and in the stages of life by Vigeland in Frogner Park, Oslo, Norway. There is a totally different feel, a different emotion.

macaroni may seem like a queer medium for sculpture, but the distinctive imagery that results is usually quite startling, often comical, and always a bit fantastic. It's sheer fun to work with!

A walk down the aisle of your

supermarket will reveal macaroni of many shapes—corkscrews, spirals, seashells, bows, ribbons, letters, even wheels. These ready-made shapes easily lend themselves to the three-dimensional techniques.

You need a piece of cardboard or wood for a base, a candle, sealing wax, an old spoon, Elmer's glue, and an interesting assortment of macaroni.

Construct the figure directly on the base, from the bottom up. First, melt a piece of the sealing wax in the spoon by holding it over the candle flame, then dip your first piece of macaroni into the sealing wax and attach it quickly, while the wax is hot, to the base. Hold it securely until the wax hardens and the piece stands by itself. Then continue the process, welding each piece of macaroni to the next until the figure is completed.

Dimensional Doodling

Sealing wax is used as the first adhesive because of the speed with which it hardens, making it possible to compose designs rapidly. Its brittleness can be overcome by later applying Elmer's glue to every joint.

Caution: Welding with sealing wax should be done when the wax flows easily back and forth as the spoon is tilted. Sealing wax is inflammable. If it catches fire while you are melting, quickly remove it from the candle flame and blow the fire out.

Toothpicks may be used instead of macaroni. Though an amateur's medium, toothpick sculpture reminds one of the stainless steel *Construction with Thirty Identical Elements,* a gracefully balanced piece of sculpture by Max Bill.

Soda straws could also be used.

these move with the breeze

Mobiles which hang and move and stabiles which stand and move are intriguing in their construction because of their delicate balance. Wire may be used as the basic structure to which you attach paper, aluminum, plastic, or styrofoam pieces. The mobile is built from the bottom up in a free-moving form; the stabile has a base from which the construction is begun. Alexander Calder has a delightful mobile *Red Petals.* Patience is the key as you work with the intricate and delicate balance of a mobile or a stabile.

wrap it up!

Stovepipe, newspaper baling wire, insulated wire, copper wire, aluminum wire, stiff wire, easy-to-bend wire, red, blue, green, white wire pipe cleaners, or clothes hangers. Choose the kind of wire that feels most comfortable to you.

Form a large and simple shape first by twisting and bending it into the form you have in mind. If you don't like what you've made, straighten it out and start over again. You may wrap wire around pencils, sticks, bottles, or small boxes for different effects, but you should be able to

remove the object after you have finished if you later decide you wish to do so.

Bent wire can be left in a simple shape and mounted on a base of wood with glue or staples. Alexander Calder's *Sow,* which is on exhibit in the Museum of Modern Art, is a very simple outline of wire, yet very artistic in its ryhthm.

You may want to coil wire around the torso of the figure as loosely or as tightly as you desire, developing a cocoon-like feeling in places. Use finer wire for this process. Tie as needed to hold the shape firm and to prevent slipping of major wires from their place. Changes in shape can be made at any point simply by giving a twist or indenting with a push. Keep the work open enough to see the underlying sculpture. Keep in mind the element of surprise so that from every point of viewing you can see through the sculpture to the other side.

crush & form

Who could imagine that the sleek roll of shiny thin metal which we use every day in the kitchen could have another more entertaining use—sculpturing. It has its limitations, but its possibilities and

advantages outweigh them. Available and cheap, clean and mess-free, it can be worked anywhere and by hand without any tools. Aluminum foil is great!

After choosing a subject, visualize its general form. Do not try to complete any one area first, but get the general form and go back and do the details. Crumple any extra material underneath to add strength and volume. Extra foil may be added as stuffing to help keep the contour of the design. Don't overwork the foil. Once crushed it cannot be reused successfully. Allow for such things as appendages on animals and crumple them into place at the proper time. Beginners may find heavy duty foil easier to work. You may need to patch here and there with extra foil, but soon modeling from a single piece of foil will be an achievement. These "creatures" make wonderful mobiles. Hang with colorless, nylon thread.

Picasso called his sculpturing a kind of three-dimensional doodling, a device he used to work out ideas he intended to paint in oil. But critics have called them the "doodles of a genius." Why don't you try your hand at three-dimensional doodling? You'll find it's fun!

Aluminum foil is great for sculpture! Here is one artist crumbling forms from foil. Where will imagination take her?

Bring the Outdoors In

"Bring the outdoors in" is a modern American architectural slogan. Sliding glass doors provide a view of a patio, roof garden, or balcony where small trees, blooming flowers, and climbing vines produce the feel of natural surroundings even in the heart of a concrete city.

This approach is only a variation of what the Japanese have been doing for hundreds of years. Where farms are measured by *tsubo* (a six-by-six-foot square) and rooms by *tatami* mats (three feet by six feet) there is neither room nor material to waste. So, lacking a garden with full-scale trees to contemplate, the Japanese turned to dwarf trees. They started collecting trees that had been dwarfed by nature. The collecting developed into cultivating. Bonsai (bone-sigh), an ancient art of producing artificially dwarfed trees, probably originating in China, was introduced into Japan before the twelfth century and became popular in the seventeenth century.

As living space becomes more crowded and natural things farther removed from us, bonsai and glass gardens are gaining in popularity as persons yearn to watch things grow and to feel the relaxation that comes from working with nature.

Instant Bonsai, the American way

The Japanese think of a tree as a dear companion. Families keep the same dwarf tree for many generations. Some are known to be over three hundred years old. A harried American asked a bonsai grower, "But doesn't it take a lot of patience?" The Japanese answered, "Patience is needed only by those who don't enjoy what they are doing."

Before your family begins a bonsai project, notice how a tree struggles to adjust to its environment. Wind, sun, moisture, soil—all have their effects. Some trees give the impression of quiet and peace. Some tell a thrilling story of survival against the elements. You can produce the same effect in miniature.

Decide the Effect You Want

Is the tree to give a sense of peace and calm or of struggle and courage? Is it to bloom or bear fruit? These considerations will govern not only the kind of tree but the container as well.

Small pine, junipers, or cedar trees make excellent bonsai. The colorful pyracantha, rhododendron, and azaleas work well. Look carefully for seedling trees sprouting along fences, near older trees, or close to rocks.

To discover hidden possibilities, lift the plant up to eye level and look at main branches, disregarding the twiggy stems. Remove all surplus growth to expose the principal trunk, or trunks, and branches. Pruning is mainly a matter of revealing the basic structure of the plant. Make cuts clean.

Pot It Up

Cleanly cut off overlong roots and shorten others by a third. Remove some of the tops to balance the loss. Cover drainage holes in the container to prevent soil from sifting through. Equal amounts of good garden soil, sand, and peat moss make a suitable potting mix which should be poked down among the roots. Tap the pot occasionally to settle the soil. Water with fine spray.

To Change the Shape

To change or help the shape of your tree use soft copper wire—pliable and rustproof. Insert the wire into the soil close to the trunk. Wind it up and around both the trunk and the branches, being careful not to damage the bark. The wire can be removed in six months.

Good Luck and Good Pruning!

Bonsai is a Japanese word that literally means "tray planting." It is intended to suggest a whole landscape,

condensing all of nature into one tiny tree
and its setting of a bit of moss and a rock
or two. In shaping plants, just about
anything can happen. It's up to you.
Do begin but do be careful.
It is so hard not to make room
for just one more!

See-through gardens

If you have a yen for greenery indoors
but a limited time for care of house plants,
why not try a see-through garden?
Arranging plants in jars or bottles was,
and still is, a fine art—a pleasure to do
and a delight to see!

Almost any plant can grow successfully under glass. The secret is to choose
varieties that have the same light and
moisture requirements.

Planting Materials

Basic cover: bromeliad, maidenhair,
fern, marantas, fittonias, selaginella.
For color: miniature geraniums, begonias,
gloxinias, silvery-leafed philodendron,
African violets, oleander.
Others: vinca (tall), tiny baby's tears,
dwarf palm, small-leafed ivies.

Getting Ready to Plant

See-through gardens are fun to put
together; they are a snap to care for!
Small-necked containers take more
patience, but you are rewarded, for they
make excellent conversation pieces.
Whatever container you choose—a tall
bottle; a large, flat one; a brandy snifter;
or a squatty boiling flask—make it shine
with glass cleaner. To prevent soiling
the sides with dirt, coil a newspaper
into a funnel that will fit all the way
inside the bottle to within an inch
of the bottom.

If you want a "parfait" look in the
soil (especially attractive in tall bottles),
carefully put in layers of fine pebbles,
charcoal, crushed clay pots, and good dark
earth. For more shallow containers use
pebbles and some charcoal as a base to
keep the soil sweet and to help it drain
properly. For an interesting effect in a
larger container create a slope so the plants
in the rear are slightly higher than
those in the front.

Placing Plants in Position

You will need sheets of wax paper,
a long piece of wire (a part of a clothes
hanger works fine), and a chopstick-like
utensil. Carefully remove most of the soil
from each plant. Gently coil each plant
in a piece of wax paper, furling it small
enough to fit through the bottle neck.
Slip the coiled paper inside and shake
lightly to release the plant. Remove the
paper and begin work with wire and sticks.
Place plant in upright position, in
approximately the place where you want it.
Then, using the paper funnel, add just
enough soil about the roots to hold it in
place.

Repeat until all the plants are inside
and then begin maneuvering them with
your tools, adding soil as necessary to hold
everything in place. Cover all the roots
with about one half inch of soil. Do not
crowd the plantings. Tamp soil firmly
around roots.

When all plants are placed, add
swatches of moss or other basic cover,
first working them down along the side,
between the soil and the glass, moss side
out. Then cover all spaces around the
plants, carefully working the moss around
the stem bases. Water slightly.

Set in a place that has bright light
but little or no direct sun. If soil appears
dry and plants droop, add a bit of water.
If glass becomes misty, remove cover
for a while.

If you seal the top, you have created
a microenvironment that almost never
needs help from the outside. Add
a few insects (flies, mosquitoes, beetles,
or crickets) and a small animal
(frog or lizard), and you have a
miniature life support system which
children enjoy!

Nature's Own Paints and Beads

Celebrate the earth...

Rachel Carson in *The Sense of Wonder* writes, "If a child is to keep alive his inborn sense of wonder . . . he needs the companionship of at least one adult who can share it, rediscover with him the joy, excitement, and mystery of the world we live in."

Walk into the out-of-doors on a warm April day. Lift a stone and watch the beetles, centipedes, millipedes, earwigs, earthworms scurry from the light and your intrusion. Make sure you replace the rock for some of those tiny creatures cannot live long exposed to light and heat.

Stop and watch the ants carrying loads bigger than their bodies, a wasp building its nest, a spider spinning a web, an earthworm burrowing in the soil, a bee gathering nectar from a flower blossom, or a seed sprouting in the garden.

Go to a wooded area and listen to the singing of birds and insects. Observe their busy activities. How do you feel as you stand quietly there? What colors do you see? What do you think causes you to feel as you do? Have you felt this way before? What evidences have you seen that man is destroying much of our natural beauty?

As you ride through the countryside, what things do you see that detract from beauty? How is much of the land being used? In the city, are there ugly areas? What do you see that obstructs the view of the sky? How do you feel about it all?

Discuss with children the ways that each individual can not only develop environmental awareness, but can do something about what he sees, hears, smells, and tastes that he does not feel is contributing to the benefit of the *whole* earth.

Needed: a new kind of person...

who views all of life on earth as fundamentally good,
  who condemns any effort to destroy life,
    who senses the sacredness and holiness of the earth,
      who realizes the dependence of all creatures on each other
          for life itself,
     who recognizes a relationship to the environment
not as
    economic gain,
      increased productivity,
         greater consumption of goods, or
           easier and more comfortable living,
but as
    a precious gift of God to us,
      entrusted to our care and keeping.

Use nature's gifts...

Paints. When you are walking along the street or along a stream, look for soft, colored stones which can be used to make natural paint, just as the Indians once did. You'll find these stones in parking lots as well as in the bed of small streams. Grind the soft stones into a fine powder, using hard flat stones as grinding tools. Grind with a circular motion and add small amounts of water until a rather thick paste is formed.

After several colors have been made, you are ready for Indian painting. With your fingers or a feather, paint your face as the Indians do for their ceremonial dances or celebrations. To get different colors, try mixing two paints.

Dyes. The early pioneers didn't have Rit or Tintex dyes which you can buy in a store. They used herbs and berries which grew nearby to make their own dyes.

Did you know that marigold blossoms make a lovely yellow dye? Onion skins a bright orange? Get out your old white T-shirts, blouses, and shirts. Experiment by dyeing them with nature's own brilliant colors.

Boil the vegetable matter *at least* one hour. Strain the liquid through a clean cloth. Then dip the material you have ready to dye in the liquid. Remember that the different boiling times change the intensity of the color so you may get several shades of the same color.

For dyes:

Yellow: Marigold and golden Marguerite blossoms, milkweed

Orange: The papery brown skin of common cooking onions

Red: Dahlia and zinnia petals

Lilac blue: Fruit of the native elderberry

Brown: Black walnut hulls soaked overnight, then boiled

For tie dyeing pull up a shape in the cloth resembling a rabbit ear. Separate the rabbit ear from the flat cloth by tightly tying it with string at its base. Wrap the string around it many times. The wider the band of string, the wider the circle will be.

Experiment with scrap material before trying the pattern on your shirt. A tip: Old cotton material dyes best. Man-made synthetics are very difficult to dye.

Beads are in...

Nature's beads. Melon, pumpkin, and squash seeds must be washed, then soaked overnight. While wet they can be pierced with a needle and strung on nylon fishing line or heavy waxed thread.

Eucalyptus pods, cloves, and allspice can be soaked overnight and pierced with a needle, making a very fragrant necklace. Pierce the cloves through the stem.

Clay beads. Clay beads are simple to make. Form clay into little balls and make a hole in each one with a nail. Smooth with water, dry, and then fire, if a kiln is available. Instead of glazing them, you can mosaic them with tiny, smooth pebbles. Use epoxy glue to secure them on the clay.

Flower leis. Our Hawaiian friends greet us with flower leis and "Aloha." Children make leis from clover blossoms and dandelion stems. Why don't you "celebrate" the good earth by making a colorful lei from her treasures? ☐

Tie Them in Knots

There are creative possibilities in the practical knot

When we become aware of all the fascinating things around us, we wonder, "Why do we want to work with our ugly, machine-made stuff instead of the lovely growing things outside our door?" Or, "Why buy things to work and play with when so many exciting things enter our door but are tossed away?" Look around and you will find the materials needed for macramé, the ancient art of creating with knots.

Knotting has appeared in most cultures in one form or another. The early macramé was used primarily as a finishing touch on the edge of a piece

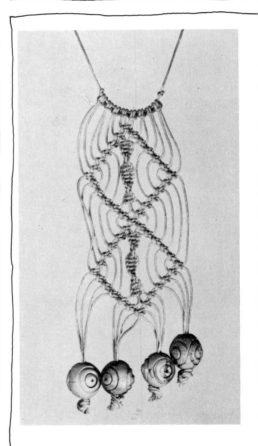

Some knots...

Half Knot

Square Knot

Double Half Hitch

BReaK iNTo THE UNeXPeCTeD!

" 'Freedom' is not the right to live as we wish; it is the right to learn how we *ought* to live in order to fulfill all our potentialities," wrote Sidney J. Harris. Thomas Carlyle worded it a bit differently:

> The great law of culture is:
> Let each become all that
> he was created
> capable of being;
> expand, if possible to
> his full growth; and show
> himself at length in his own
> shape and stature
> be these what they may.

God has created almost limitless potentialities within his world and within man. He has great faith in man, for he gave us the freedom to use our abilities wisely or unwisely. As in the parable of the talents (or use of abilities) many of us fail to develop all that is within us because we are afraid to venture, to risk failure, to do something different, or to be persons uniquely ourselves. We never see beyond the routine, the obvious, the everydayness of life. We muddle through our existence as if living were a chore, something to be endured, never acknowledging each new day as a gift from God.

"It is a known fact," writes Alex F. Osborn in *Applied Imagination,* "that nearly all of us can become more creative, if we will. And this very fact may well be the hope of the world. By becoming more creative we can lead brighter lives, and can live better with each other. . . . By becoming more creative we may even find a way to bring permanent peace to all the world." He goes on to say, "To cease to think and live creatively is but little different from ceasing to live."

When we do break out of the ordinary and comfortable and venture into the unexpected and untried, we may discover a certain kind of beauty or simplicity or harmony or spiritual involvement. We may feel some of the same ecstasy and exhilaration experienced by the psalmist (103:1) and respond:

"Bless the Lord, O my soul;
    and all that is within me, bless
      his holy name!"
and declare our faithfulness to him:
"I will sing to the Lord as long as I
    live;
I will sing praise to my God
    while I have being" (Psalm
    104:33).

of woven material. Knotted textiles were used as fringes on costumes of Babylonian and Assyrian sculptures. The earliest knotted textures that have survived (and are preserved at the Kircheriano Museum in Rome) are game bags and nets used for catching wild animals.

Most people, however, associate macramé with more decorative items made of rope and cord by early sailors who spent long hours tying knots. Boy Scouts have also preserved and encouraged the art of knot tying. Though their skill in tying knots is applied in very practical ways, the same knots used for securing a boat or pitching a tent may be used for decorative purposes.

The equipment and materials needed for macramé are not elaborate. Some cord or twine, scissors, a few pins and a work surface are all that is really needed. You may enjoy rummaging through the basement or attic for discarded strings — rug yarn, cotton wrapping twine, cable cord, rayon cord, jute, fish line, seine net — which can be used successfully.

Beads, pieces of wood, shells, soda can pull-tabs, metal washers, wooden beads, cork pieces, steel springs may be incorporated into macramé wall hangings for emphasis and interest. To obtain a three-dimensional sculptural effect, knotted pieces can be built over a framework of wood or wire.

Don't be discouraged by complex illustrations or directions given in popular magazines. You need only a basic "repertoire" of three or four knots to achieve a great deal of variety. The overhand knot, or half hitch, that everyone does automatically can be your first step. The square knot is familiar. The double half hitch and the clover hitch make for a more elaborate pattern. Then there are the intriguing ones: the fisherman's bend, the granny knot, the cat's paw, figure eight, and the true lover's knot.

A small wall hanging is a good beginning project because it is large enough to try several designs and small enough so it does not become too fatiguing before it is completed. To begin, cut as many lengths of the cord as are needed to make the desired width for the hanging. Double each cord and make a loop over a dowel pin or small tree branch. Pull each of the double strands through the loops and tighten around the hanging device. From there begin to tie knots which make a pleasing effect to you. Pins stuck through the cord into the working surface help to hold the hanging in place while you are tying.

Belts, bib necklaces, and chokers are popular with youth. In making jewelry, clusters of beads in soft colors are used with a waxed linen cord or rattail, a satin-covered cord. The designs may be more symmetrical and, because of the fineness of the cord used, appear to be more intricate, but the same basic knots are used.

A macramé project — newly begun

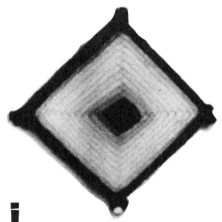

If macramé is not your "cup of tea," why not make a design, made with yarn, called "God's Eye"? Originally "God's Eye" was a symbol of protection for the Huichol Indians. We first saw it in Taos, New Mexico, when we visited the pueblos near the city. Later, in the Chicago-O'Hare terminal building, we noticed a college girl carrying a lovely large wall hanging with this design woven on small tree branches.

For a small "God's Eye" design, take two toothpicks (or used matches, even small twigs) and with yarn tie the two toothpicks together in the middle and at right angles to each other. Begin by wrapping the yarn under a toothpick, and then up and around it. Continue weaving your way around the toothpick frame until it is filled. Form a loop for hanging and tie securely.

For a larger design, use something longer than toothpicks — dowel pins, small tree branches. For a variety in the design weave under the frame for several rounds and then come up *over* the frame and then around it, to finish out. Two colors also produce an interesting effect. The small designs may be hung on trees at Christmastime, on mobiles. Larger ones make nice wall hangings.

All my life I have been intrigued by the process of weaving, from admiring a friend's artistry on the loom in her home to marveling at the vast amount of material turned out on the commercial looms at Front Royal, Va.

Everywhere I go I am fascinated by the variety of patterns, designs, textures, and products of the weaving art — the delicate silk of Italy, the lovely, woolen sweaters of Norway, the tiny, lacey baskets of Madeira, the intricate Khus grass coasters of Curacao, the sturdy, open baskets of Gran Canaria, the colorful table mats of Hawaii, the huge floor mats of Nigeria and the heavy, coarse rugs of Navajoland. Each has a distinctive charm of its own. Each reflects the native material of its area. Each shows the creativity and the ingenuity of its people.

Nosing around in a library, I found some unique but simple weaving ideas. I have had fun experimenting with them. I hope you will too.

soda straws?

The everyday drinking straw offers an opportunity to become acquainted with the weaving process with a different kind of "loom." Straws can be the framework to hold the warp — the series of threads that lie in a vertical position. Narrow or wide forms, made by using varied numbers of straws as the framework to hold the warp, may be woven into colorful belts, interesting ties, and striking wall hangings.

You will need: straws (drinking or soda), scissors, string, yarn

More fancy materials: ribbon, cords, tinsel, fabric cut in strips, thick and thin yarns, multicolored yarns

Directions for straw weaving: Cut drinking straws in half and cut one warp string for each straw. Strings should be equal in length and as long as you wish the finished product to be. Tie all the warp strings together in a knot. Place the knotted end of the warp at the top of the straws. (Suck on the straw to get the string through easily.) Push the straws up to the knotted ends. Weave over and under the straws, beginning a pattern.

Add new color by tying a knot to the previous color and continue weaving. As the weaving process progresses, push the woven section up and off the warp when the weaving is finished. Weave the end strings into one another so they will not ravel.

For variety, use several strands of warp through each straw. Since this provides for additional warp threads, more intricate weaving is possible. Vary the materials used for weft — the horizontal threads used for weaving over and under the warp — using some of the optional materials suggested. Use pieces of the straw as part of the finished design. Sew completed pieces into new forms, or superimpose them on a burlap background.

wire? chicken wire?

You will need: wire screen, such as window screen, chicken wire, hardware cloth (hail screen); yarn; string; wire cutters; scissors; needles; masking tape

Other materials: burlap, straw, beads, ribbon, pipe cleaners, tissue paper, weed, felt, raffia

Weaving in wire mesh, using a variety of types and strips of fabrics, opens some fresh avenues for creative expression. Since wire comes in a variety of meshes, you can choose the size of mesh that you wish to try your hand at. You can manipulate the wire into three-dimensional shapes, cut out parts, or (to create a multidimensional effect) superimpose cut-out areas over a screen of a different mesh.

Each kind of wire mesh has its own possibilities and limitations as a background for weaving. In addition, you will want to be sensitive to color, texture

Out with Soda Straws

and pattern. The simple over-under process of weaving into mesh can result in very unusual and effective designs. You experiment and explore with your own artistic ideas in mind.

Directions: Cut the wire and bind it with masking tape to prevent scratches. Begin to weave materials into the mesh background. As the weaving progresses, analyze the weaving for design qualities. View it from a distance, or if a sculptural form, at different angles.

You may want to use a pre-planned design by placing the wire shape on paper and drawing around it. With a crayon draw a design on the paper. Place the wire mesh over the design and with a felt marker, trace the design onto the wire.

Of the three most common wire meshes, chicken wire is probably the easiest to work with. You can span and connect areas of yarn by tying or weaving fibers in and around the wire. Window screen, a finer mesh, suggests the use of threads and finely textured yarn for designing. Hardware cloth seems to call for thick yarns and bulky fabrics.

Each wire mesh can be accented by using paint sprays of gold or bronze.

a cardboard loom?

You will need: heavy cardboard, string, yarn, scissors, ruler

More fancy materials: ribbon, crepe paper; can you think of others?

Method I: Draw a line along the top and bottom of the cardboard, which has been cut to the size of the finished product, about one half inch from the edge. Cut slits from edge to this line, about a half inch apart. Anchor the warp (yarn) in the top slits and stretch to the bottom of the cardboard. Pull through the notch, around to the next notch on the bottom, up to the top, until it is strung in all the notches. With this method, you will weave on only one side of the cardboard.

Method II: Attach the warp to a cardboard frame. This permits working from both front and back of the weaving. Cut four strips of cardboard. Make slits in the two pieces used for top and bottom of the frame. Be careful that there are

an equal number of slits on each. Staple the four pieces of cardboard together to form a frame, pointing slits outward so they serve as notches through which the warp can be looped. Pull the warp just tight enough so that it will lie flat on the frame. Proceed to weave the design within the frame.

Method III. Cut a circle of cardboard, slit around the edges and around a hole which has been cut in the center. The warp is anchored in the slits and

wrapped around both sides of the circle. Each side is woven independently and the cardboard stays in the middle. This is especially good for weaving mats for hot dishes.

Note: The device for holding the warp may be slits, notches or pins stuck in the end of the cardboard.

Kinds of weaves:
Tabby weave: over one and under one
Twill weave: over one and under two
Basket weave: over two and under two

**Children of yesterday, heirs of tomorrow,
What are you weaving? Labor and sorrow?
Look to your looms again; faster and faster
Fly the great shuttles prepared by the Master.
Life's in the loom! Room for it, room!**

MARY ARTEMISIA LATHBURY

To Cook Is to Tell a Story

To cook is to tell a story, for it recreates the past. Many of the recipes being used today were not written down but handed down, like folk ballads, mouth to mouth, memory to memory.

Food is exciting! A woman who feels that there is excitement in preparing and serving food and who invests a bit of charm in the most unpretentious meal brings a special something to the happiness of her family for, as Samuel Pepys wrote three hundred years ago, it is "strange to see how a good dinner and feasting reconciles everybody." How often in tense situations the walls come tumbling down when a family gets together over a special meal!

Mealtime is also a time for forming lasting habits of good conduct and for teaching social graces to growing boys and girls. Might it be that the "eat and run" habit of many children today is due to an inferred lack of caring in the serving of frozen and precooked foods that require no more preparation than flicking on an electric oven?

In each person there is a desire to create something, because it is only through producing something that is peculiarly one's own that a person can become distinctive. Few of us achieve distinction through creating a role in a play or through painting a picture or writing a piece of music, but every woman can say to herself, "As I prepare this meal I am creating something," for every time she sets a table she creates a picture, a mood.

Meal planning is a game that's fun if you play it with imagination and zest. It is important to plan well-balanced meals, but it is equally important to make these meals appetizing and attractive with plenty of variety. Cooking is an art that should delight the senses. The Chinese suggest that a well-prepared dish of food should appeal to the eye by its coloring, to the nose by its aroma, to the ear by its sounds

(crunch, crunch), and, of course, to the mouth by its flavor. The Chinese would feel sorry for the families who are victims of "Link sausage! Not again!" for they know over 250 ways to cook pork alone! So, add a Cinderella touch to some of your basic dishes—sprinkle a bit of nutmeg atop a baked custard, shake a dash of cinnamon on an apple pie, drop a few snips of chives or parsley on a bowl of soup, brush the top of a pie crust with milk for that golden glazed finish, or spank that cookie with a fork and make it pretty as well as tasty.

When cooking shifts from being a necessity to an art, the kitchen itself seems to change from a sterile utilitarian room to a place with a personality. It is no longer a status symbol, looking like a picture in a woman's magazine, but it will be known chiefly by its fragrances and its clutter. There will be carrots and onions laying on the counters, fruit ripening in bowls on the table, something savory baking in the oven. Long-handled forks, wooden spoons, pots and pans of all shapes will fill the sink. It might not be neat; it won't even look efficient. But when you enter you will feel a sense of "at-homeness," for the cook in this home appreciates the beauty of tomatoes to be peeled, enjoys the smell of peaches to be canned, relishes the snap of green beans, and delights in the feel of kneading bread. She finds satisfaction in the everyday tasks of the kitchen. Or, as Josephine Moffett Benton says in *Pace of a Hen:*

> "It isn't stuffing a turkey and peeling onions, and washing celery; it is preparing food to place before people to remind them of all their unearned blessings on this day. Then there's a high joy in having the food my strength and care have produced become a source of strength to those I love. In that way—a mystical thing perhaps—I become part of them."

Food has a special meaning to children. A tiny baby cries; his mother feeds him. The feel of warm milk flowing into an empty stomach and the comfort of being cozily held brings emotional satisfactions as well. What started out to be a physical response soon carries deeper meanings.

I recall many childhood impressions and associations with food. My grandmother with a bowl of crisp, red apples in her lap peeled an apple 'round and 'round. I watched with fascination as the long curl fell in a graceful spiral from her hands. The deft hands of my husband's mother, fluting the crust of a pie in an artistic way all her own, were those of a master of the art.

My mother, who felt the sacred in the commonplace, passed this awe to me as we planted seeds in the warm, moist earth, watched them grow and mature, appreciated the abundant harvest, preserved the surplus, and later enjoyed the taste of spring when the wintry winds blew.

All of these tasks spelled love to me, for they were done in the spirit of joy and self-giving.

As a child observes adult activities he tries out everything he sees them do. Sometimes the "helping" results in being told to stay out of the way or not to bother until mother is finished. But food and love are linked together by the Nigerian baby on the back of his mother as she grinds the guinea corn for gruel, and by Lois's family when she grinds the wheat into flour and bakes beautiful, crusty loaves of bread for them to eat. A child misses out on a lot of fun if he thinks peas come from boxes and corn from plastic bags!

Use fresh vegetables, growing and picking them, if possible. Encourage your child to feel and taste the raw vegetables while you are preparing them for the table. Let him help when it is safe. Make butter by simply shaking cream in a covered jar. As you are making soup, play a game of identifying the various ingredients by touch, smell, or taste. Help him make jello, cube it when set, and place in parfait glasses or custard cups. He will enjoy the sparkle. Cookies—mixing, cutting, baking, and decorating them—make an excellent project for the two of you.

Perhaps even a mistake will result in a "new creation," for tradition has it that a careless monk made too much dough. Since he had been warned against waste-fulness, he twisted some of the strips into the shape of arms folded in prayer. To the youngster who was best at reciting prayers he said, "Here's a reward for saying your prayers faithfully and without mistakes." Before long he was baking "pretiolas" (Latin for "little reward") by the dozens. When we visited America's oldest pretzel bakery in Lititz, Pennsylvania, we were told that "There's a prayer in every pretzel."

In *The Practice of the Presence of God,* Brother Lawrence said,

"The time of business does not with me differ from the time of prayer; and in the noise and clutter of my kitchen . . . I possess God in as great tranquility as if I were upon my knees. . . ."

To cook is to tell a story—or to breathe a prayer.

"I can make any kind of figure I want to," said Mrs. Johnie Head confidently as she fingered the corn husks on the table. In the lean year of 1934 Mrs. Head had worried about Christmas gifts for their children. One day while looking at the corn which grew outside her door a brainstorm flashed through her mind. "Why can't I make dolls for the girls and animals for the boys from those corn husks?"

As a result of her skill she has created hundreds and hundreds of corn husk "people" and animals. So proficient and artistic has this Arkansas woman become that she was invited to the Smithsonian Folk Art Festival in 1968 and again in 1969. There she demonstrated her folk art which she does now "to pass away the lonesome time."

The ingenuity of Mrs. Head is characteristic of people through the ages, for dolls have been fashioned from whatever was available.

Children Everywhere Have Dolls

Indians and Eskimos made wooden, clay, applehead, ivory, and bone dolls as playthings for their children. New England mothers made dolls out of stuffed stockings, cornhusks, paper, and gingerbread. A pioneer woman might make a cloth body for a doll, and the father would carve a wooden head and paint on a face and curls. The Kachina dolls resemble kachina dancers who perform in Hopi Indian ceremonies.

Stuffed Dolls

When mothers made the simple stuffed dolls at home, they cut out two matching pieces of cloth and stitched the front and back of a doll together, leaving a slit at the bottom. Rags, sawdust, husks, or beans were stuffed into the body before the bottom was closed. A bit of paint or some stitches on the face, buttons or shells for eyes, some yarn for hair, and presto! A doll! It was dragged around by a leg or an arm and lovingly cradled in tiny, warm arms. Even plain stockings were stuffed for dolls, with hair and a mouth and eyes stitched on.

Bedraggled rag dolls were not thrown away but were often covered with a clean cloth for younger children. Many such dolls outlived their first owners.

Nuthead Dolls

Seeing hickory nuts scattered over the ground in the fall, an imaginative person saw tiny "faces" looking up. Thus the nuthead doll was born.

Paint the "face" on the hickory nut. Add a beard and/or hair of cotton, yarn, or raveled rope. For the body, braid three pipe cleaners. Wind "arms" around the body and extend at both sides. Wind cleaners around body below and let hang down for legs. Insert braided pipe cleaner "neck" in hole which has been made in the nut. Dress doll as you like.

If you use English walnuts, remove the meat from the two halves. Paint eyes, nose, and mouth on one half of walnut shell with a fine brush dipped in poster paint. When the face is dry, paint hair around face and on the other walnut shell, which will be the back of the head. Follow the directions above for making the body. To fasten body to head, put braided pipe cleaner "neck" inside the hollow walnut shell and glue the two halves together around the braid. Dress doll in some original way.

Clothespin Doll

The first clothespin doll is said to have originated in a Quaker settlement in New York when the clothespins were hand-carved, crudely shaped, and about six inches tall. With felt-tip markers paint features and hair on the clothespin "head." Glue the middle of a pipe cleaner across the back of the clothespin just below the "neck." Fold back one half inch at ends of pipe cleaner to make hands.

For a simple dress as made by the early Quakers, fold a piece of tracing paper in half lengthwise. Lay fold along the dotted line and trace from the pattern shown. While paper is still folded cut out tracing. Open it and you have a dress pattern. From the pattern cut fabric and sew up side seams. Hem the bottom. Cut a short slash down from the neck opening so you can put the dress on the doll. Sew a few stitches at the neck opening to keep it closed. Tie a ribbon around the waist for a sash.

Yarn Doll

These soft, cuddly dolls are a snap to make. From cardboard, cut an eight-inch square, the form for making the body, and a six-inch square to make the arms. For the body, wind the yarn about fifty times around the "body square"; for the arms about thirty times around the "arm square." Slide the body off the cardboard and tie off the top of the head, making a neck. Slide the yarn off the "arm" form and tie off both ends for hands. Then, slide the arms through the body and tie the body at the waist.

To make a boy, separate the bottom section into two bunches and tie off to make legs and feet. For a girl, clip the bottom into fringe. Make facial features from construction paper or cloth and glue into place. Add an apron or overalls for a finishing touch.

Corn Dolly

Children of the early settlers played with dolls made from corn husks and corn cobs. Although the craft was learned primarily from the Indians, the idea was an adaptation of a Scottish tradition of the kern maiden, a doll made from the last corn harvested each year.

A corn dolly takes longer to make, for, as with the applehead dolls, it must dry thoroughly. Take a fresh ear of corn with the husks still on. Pull husks back from corn cob, but do not tear them off. Carefully remove the corn silk and lay in a pile with strands smoothed straight. Tie thread around the middle of the strands. Using a kitchen knife, scrape the corn kernels off the cob and replace the husk.

Now wrap a rubber band around the cob about a third of the way down from the top. Fold the husks above the rubber band down around the cob, arrange smoothly and place another rubber band around the cob near the folded top of the husk. Put cob and silk in sun and air to dry. This may take about two weeks.

When the cob is dry, use the corn silk for the doll's hair. Put glue over the end of the cob head and arrange silk on top and sides of the head. For pigtails tie the hair at the sides with thread. Thumb-tacks may be pushed into the corn cob for eyes. Paint mouth with a felt-tipped marker. A bow around the rubber bands at the neck, a feather in a fancy headband, and Indian designs painted on the corn husk "skirt" make a clever corn dolly.

The best-loved dolls are not always the "store" dolls which shut their eyes, wet their diapers, walk, or talk. Often a preference is shown for the raggedy one, soft to the cheek, or the one unique in "character," or perhaps the one which, for some unexplained reason, is simply the "favorite." Children everywhere *need* a doll.

DRESS PATTERN

SLASH

Fun with Words

Words Words word^s – st^A|e st^{UP}id d^{U}LL t^{e}dio^{U}s Words Word^S wo^{r}Ds

tumbling over each other without thought
bubbling out with expected enthusiasm
effervescing over commonplace trivia
sickening with polite, insincere compliments
babbled incoherently and indifferently
in a world where it doesn't matter
for no one really listens anyway.
Words taped, words stored, words replayed, repeated.
Words heard, words spoken, words written.
Words, words, words! Will there be no end?

Adapting Alex F. Osborn's suggestions of ways to stretch creative thinking as it relates to things, James A. Smith in *Creative Teaching of the Language Arts in the Elementary School* (Allyn and Bacon, 1967) suggests ways to stretch the imagination in relation to words.

1. We can describe it as it is.
2. We can describe it as we feel it.
3. We can compare it to something else.
4. We can try to see it as something else.
5. We can expand our ideas.
6. We can look at it as a symbol.

As an exercise take the word *silence* through these steps. Or *laughter*. Try *loneliness*. Place an apple or a flower or a squash on the table and describe it, using these guidelines to more creative thinking. Soon the ordinary is expressed in extraordinary ways.

This exploration may be carried on anywhere and everywhere. By yourself, as a game with a friend, or as an activity for the family. Here are some tips for exploring, expanding, expressing.

But, thank goodness, occasionally you hear a person say something in such a beautiful way that you see a picture in your mind that you cannot forget. Do you remember something which was said so beautifully or so differently that you almost shivered with delight at the thought of it? Who can forget Carl Sandburg's "The fog comes on little cat feet" or the child's "Boy, is that Jello nervous!" Words can be delightful, picturesque, and memorable if we cultivate the desire and the art to make them so.

Hughes Mearns, in *Creative Power: The Education of Youth in the Cre-ative Arts* (Dover, 1958), writes, "Creative work may be known by its signal mark of originality; the genuine creative product is always an expression of one's own inimitable individuality. Maybe you talk and laugh like your age-group; if you were more creative you would talk and laugh like yourself. You, the real creative you, has no duplicate in the wide world."

Have you ever felt emotionally moved by a beautiful formation of clouds and wanted to express your feelings to a friend but felt embarrassed at trying? What makes us feel timid as adults at expressing ourselves emotionally or in a picturesque way? Children do not hesitate to experiment with speech just as they experiment with art materials.

As a child needs to manipulate and explore with paints, so must he manipulate and explore words, their meaning, and their uses before he can apply them to creative patterns of expression. To develop this skill, children (and adults as well) need to be presented with the kind of stimulation which evokes a creative response.

The stimulation must stir our creative imagination, so we first hunt for those words which are not really new, but are new to us. Then we begin to uncover alternatives, one by one, until we bring together thoughts and ideas which eventually form some expression which *is* new. Just as Carl Sandburg expressed an idea in a new way, so too has the child who refers to chalkboard erasures as "mistake dust."

Enjoy the sound of alliteration, the repetition of sounds in two or more neighboring words — the buzzing bumblebee, the chirping chickadee, or wild and woolly, tale of terror.

Play with words using onomatopoeia, the formation of a word which imitates the natural sound associated with the object of action involved. We hear it used every day but don't always identify it with this fascinating term. Listen! the tinkle of a bell, the hiss of a snake, the bouncing of a ball. . . .

Work crossword puzzles and make your own. Graph paper makes the making easier — if you can call it easy at all.

Take long words and find small words within them. Let's just use onomatopoeia. How many words can you find in it? Mat, open, nominate. . . Make your own rules before you start to play the game. For instance, can you use a letter more times than it appears in the word? Scoring — a 4 letter word counts 3 — makes it challenging to find big words.

Use a thesaurus. You'll find it fascinating.

Play Scrabble and similar word games.

Read "Toward More Picturesque Speech" and "It Pays to Increase Your Word Power" in the *Reader's Digest.*

Keep a dictionary handy! Look up the words you run across which you do not know.

Cut out unrelated pictures and write a story. Let each person arrange the pictures as he wishes for his story.

Make up stories using unrelated words in the order agreed upon, for example, cat, shaving cream, star, bark.

Classify words. List as many as you can. Note the change in connotation as different senses are brought into play.

Funny words — silly

Hard words — iron, marble, stop! . . .

Soft words — kind, fuzzy. . . .

Heavy words — lead, serious

Use your newfound words! Ever notice how a child, upon his discovery of a new word uses it continually for a few days? He is wise; wiser than he knows, perhaps.

What is yellow? What is gray? . . . .

"Black is . . .
  the feel of
    mud squishing through your fingers and toes
    fog sneaking in all around the city
  the sound of
    a thunder cloud when it breaks open
    a still night all around you
    a wave crashing down on the shore
    a hurricane
  the taste of
    licorice
      charcoal
        and burned toast . . .
          that's black."

    by Elizabeth Allstrom

Words, words, words!

Delicious, delightful, delirious words
  stimulating the imagination
    titillating the senses
      tantalizing the learner
        captivating the listener
          clarifying the message
in a world where people *will* listen
  if words are authentic and alive.
Words taped, words stored, words replayed, repeated.
But,
  words worth hearing,
  words worth speaking,
  words worth writing.
Thank goodness, there is no end!

Stretching Your Imagination

Kornei Chukovsky, "the wise and humorous writer who was a favorite of Soviet children" said, "The aim of the teller of fairy tales is first and foremost to teach the child humanity, to give him that wonderful ability to be stirred by somebody else's misfortune, to rejoice in another's joy, to feel for another as oneself."

Soviet Life, the only magazine circulated in the United States by reciprocal agreement between the two governments of the USA and the USSR, relates the reaction of children to the fairy tale play, *Gelsomino in the Land of Liars* by Gianni Rodari.

Little Gelsomino finds himself in a strange land where, when you want to say something nice, it turns into an insult; where forged money is considered real and real money, forged; where telling the truth is forbidden. You should see how agitated the children become. "Gelsomino, look out, the czar's hiding around the corner!" a girl cries. "Gelsomino, sock him one!" yells a boy. The Gelsomino show . . . has everything—adventure, a chase, singing and dancing. It also says that justice is the foundation of human existence. The theater does not lecture its reader or audience.

Fables, fairy tales, and folk tales take us into a world of fantasy. Some, like the story of Gelsomino, teach without preaching. Hans Christian Anderson was an artist at this. We remember his poignant account of that most beloved outcast, "The Ugly Duckling"; the story of how needless chatter can make a story grow as in "It's Absolutely True"; and the well-known tale of the vain and stupid ruler in "The Emperor's New Clothes."

Remember Aesop's Fables? The cocky hare who challenged the plodding tortoise to a race—then lost it? The crow and the pitcher where "little by little does the trick"? Or, the crow who, flattered by a fox, lost its morsel of food?

Other tales are for sheer enjoyment. Who hasn't wished he was on *The Flying Carpet* where "whoever seats himself on this carpet and wishes to be taken up and set down some place else, will in the twinkling of an eye be borne thither, no matter how many days distant or how hard to reach the place may be"? Or, what fun to imagine you're Paul Bunyan. When Paul was a boy he had the job of daybreaker. The cook sent him up on the Blue Mountains with an axe to break day. Paul was *so* quick he could always get the job done and get back to camp before daylight got there! And—just try to fathom the big bunkhouse at Paul's camp. It had eighty tiers. The men used to get to bed in balloons at night and come down in parachutes in the morning!

Tales from the Story Hat by Verna Aardema begins:

There is a storyteller in West Africa, who wears a story hat. It is a wide-brimmed hat of guinea corn straw and from its brim dangle many tiny carvings done in wood and ivory. Bits of fur, tips of feathers, and a leopard tooth intersperse the carvings.

Whoever asks for a story picks an object—and the storyteller is off on whatever tale it represents.

Friends who have been in Marrakech, Morocco, tell me that a crowd gathers in the village square each morning to hear the storyteller who adds yet another chapter to his long, fascinating, and spellbinding tale.

American folklore is rich in humor

and imagery. Do you know about the Goofus Bird which flies backward because it doesn't care where it's going? Have you heard of the Gollywhopper's Eggs which Willy Swift said would hatch into a super-bird? He was doing a brisk business until someone recognized the "eggs" as coconuts!

In all lands storytellers have gone from place to place telling their stories and gathering new ones. They were the first historians, preserving and handing down traditions of their people. A great deal can be learned about a tribe or clan from their folk tales. They interpret the natural, spiritual, and moral world in which people lived and moved. These stories then became a part of the rich cultural and social heritage. They tell about men who are clever as well as stupid, who are good as well as bad. Legends speculate as to how the cardinal got its red feathers, the crane its long legs, the robin her red breast, and how the long-tailed bear lost his tail.

Rudyard Kipling in *Just So Stories* begins some of his tales with, "This, O Best Beloved, is another story of the High and Far-Off Times . . . when the world was so new and all. . . ." And away you go on an imaginary journey with the most fantastic characters and learn how the leopard got his spots and the zebra his stripes.

In *Tall Tales from the High Hills* by Ellis Credle we meet Mr. Huggins, "a man left over from a way of life now vanished." He lived when people sat around the fire telling tales their grand-parents had passed down to them or made new ones out of half-forgotten lore. Old Hank begins with a riddle, "What is it that has a tongue but can't talk?" Then he would pause a while for your answer. "It's a wagon. A wagon's got a tongue but it can't talk. Only my wagon *could*. It heard plenty of tales."

If your "wagon" (car) could talk, what amusing family tales could it tell? Where would you like to go on the flying carpet? Can your family "hatch up" tall tales like Dr. Seuss in *Horton Hatches the Egg?* What outlandish things happen on your street? Can you outdo Dr. Seuss and the stories he tells in *And to Think I Saw It on Mulberry Street*!?

With radio and television, storytelling has become a lost art. Why don't you rediscover the land of fantasy and fun with your children? Make up a fable. Create a fairy tale. How do *you* imagine the rabbit got its "cotton tail"? And why not write your own family folk tales—true happenings as well as some imaginings. Record them or write them down so years from now people will know what it was like to live when. . . .

K. STANLEY

Poetry for Thanksgiving

"My enemies say bad things about me. . . . They gather all the bad news about me, and then go out and tell it everywhere. . . . Even my best friend, the one I trust the most, the one who shared my food, has turned against me. . . . [but] you will keep me in your presence forever," so wrote the psalmist (41:5, 6, 9, 12b, TEV). It is one of a very important but comparatively infrequent type of psalm — the individual song of thanksgiving. It is not a general one, "Thank you, God, for everything," but a "Thank you, God, for helping me through surgery." It expresses a firsthand, religious experience, a gratifying assurance that prayers are heard by God. As a result of this security, the psalmist seems to have put his complete confidence and trust in the Lord.

The ten psalms usually included in this category are 18, 30, 32, 34, 41, 66, 92, 116, 118, and 138. Let's listen to parts of these prayers (TEV):

"I prayed to the Lord and he answered me; he freed me from my fears" (34:4).

"The Lord is near to those who are discouraged; he saves those who have lost all hope" (34:18).

"I cried to you for help, Lord my God, and you healed me" (30:2).

"When I did not confess my sins, I was worn out from crying all day. Then I confessed my sins to you; . . . and you forgave my transgressions" (32:3, 5).

"Death pulled its ropes tight around me. . . . In my trouble I called to the Lord; . . . my cry for help reached his ears" (18:5, 6a).

"I was filled with anxiety and fear . . . The Lord saved me from death" (116:3b, 8a).

"You answered when I called to you; with your strength you strengthened me" (138:3).

These words have a familiar ring to them for we too have experienced sickness, fear, anxiety, discouragement, insincerity of friends, lack of strength, and guilt.

But listen again as the words of joy, gratitude, praise, and trust almost tumble over each other in exuberance and thanksgiving:

How I love you, Lord!
You have changed my sadness into a
    joyful dance; you have taken off my
    clothes of mourning, and have given
    me clothes of joy.
So I will not be silent;
    I will sing praise to you.
Lord, you are my God,
    I will give thanks to you forever.
I praise God,
    because he did not reject my prayer,
    or keep back his constant love from
    me.
I love the Lord, because he hears me;
    he listens to my prayers.
He listens to me
    every time I call to him.
Give thanks to the Lord, because he is
    good, and his love is eternal.

Your mighty acts, Lord, make me glad;
    because of what you have done I
    sing for joy.
How good it is to give thanks to the
    Lord, . . . to proclaim your constant
    love every morning, and your faith-
    fulness every night.
I will always thank the Lord;
    I will never stop praising him.
I will praise him for what he has done;
    may all who are oppressed listen
    and be glad!
Praise God with shouts of joy, all
    people!
Sing to the glory of his name;
    offer him glorious praise!
Say to God, "How wonderful are the
    things you do!"
What a wonderful day the Lord has
    given us;
    let us be happy, let us celebrate!
Proclaim with me the Lord's greatness;
    let us praise his name together!
        — Psalms 18:1; 30:11, 12; 66:
        20; 116:1, 2; 118:1; 92:4,
        1, 2; 34: 1, 2; 66:1-3a; 118:
        24; 34:3 (TEV)

"Let us praise his name together!" and "Find out for yourself how good the Lord is!" (34:8).

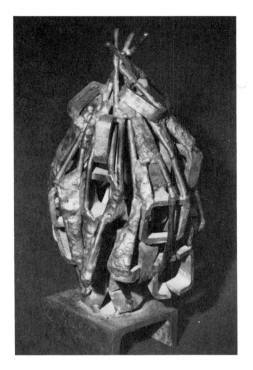

Psalm 34 is written in acrostic form. That means that if it had been written in English, the first line would have begun with A, the second with B, the third with C, until the last one would start with Z. In English it would be a twenty-six-line poem.

Since there are twenty-two letters in the Hebrew alphabet, Psalm 34 has twenty-two lines (verses). A "super-duper" acrostic occurs in the 119th Psalm, with eight lines beginning with the first letter, eight with the second, etc., making a grand total of 176 verses — the longest chapter in the Bible!

Try writing your own psalm in the acrostic form. It might begin something like this:

*A*ll day long I marveled at God's goodness,
*B*eautiful is his earth; many are our gifts.
*C*ome, praise the Lord with me!
*D*ozens of times a day I look to God
*E*ver mindful that he hears my prayers
*F*or he is a loving God.
G
H
and on to *Z*.

The chapter "Fun with Words" suggested that you experiment with words. Now, let's put words together, expressing our thanks in poetry as did the psalmist of old. We won't all be famous poets like John Ciardi or Ogden Nash or Robert Frost, but let's have some fun! Do give poetry a try!

...there's Haiku...

Haiku, a form of Japanese poetry, has seventeen syllables. The syllables are thought out carefully to express a feeling or a thought about nature. The poems are not intended to be clear statements; they are fleeting responses or impressions. Often there are three lines: the first with five syllables, the the second seven, and the third five.

Ah, leafless oak tree,
Acorns, squirrels at your feet
Thanks for summer shade.

God, our Creator,
Flowers, people — many hues;
Beautiful! Our thanks!

...or Cinquain

Cinquain (sing-kan') is a five-line verse form of two types. The first has two syllables in the first and last lines, and four, six, and eight syllables in the intervening lines.

Good earth   (2)
Luscious, ripe fruit   (4)
Pears, apples, peaches, plums   (6)
Blossoms, showers, sunshine, breezes, (8)
Our gifts!   (2)

Cinquain may be written this way: first line, the title; second line, two words to describe the title; third line, three words to express action concerning the title; fourth line, four words to express feeling about the title; fifth line, one word that means the same as the title.

Thanksgiving
Words, actions
Spoken, unspoken, demonstrated
Caring, loving, warm, tender
Thanksliving!
Happy   poetry   writing!

PUTTING IT TOGETHER

An article in *Liturgy** states:

Faith in Jesus as a way of life cannot exist without rituals, nor, in fact, can any way of life that has some basis in a conscious setting of priorities. People today can and do exist without ritual. But man without ritual is not man come of age; he is a man without age—no past to celebrate, no present to explore, no future to anticipate. No way to look at what has been, is, and will be.

Ritual in the Jewish faith dates back to the days of Moses and the covenant recorded in Deuteronomy 6:4-9. As a constant reminder of the covenant a mezuzah, which contains the Shema, is mounted on the doorpost of a Jewish home and is touched as family members come and go. Jewish children are accustomed to rituals, for as families they celebrate the Seder, Hanukkah, Yom Kippur, and many other festivals.

Though children may become accustomed to ritual as they grow up—rituals in the church, at school, and at public functions—many are quite uncomfortable with a ritual at home. Perhaps this feeling is the result of our failure to speak in deeply human words and gestures which give relationships and atmosphere the warm, personal touch which makes children feel at home with a song sung together or a common prayer at mealtime.

IMPORTANT: AUTHENTICITY

Today there is a searching for a sincere ritual (worship) within the Christian family. The rediscovery of the need for and the power inherent in ritual seems again to be something to celebrate in life. In spite of the problems of living there is a wonderfulness in reality, and this feeling of joy needs expression. It is a natural that it be expressed in the family. For, as Evelyn Duvall notes in *Faith in Families,* "The family is important

**Liturgy,* vol. 15, no. 6 (June, 1970), p. 13. (The Liturgical Conference, Washington, D. C.).

because it shapes us. More than any other force, it determines the kind of people we are and the kind of people tomorrow's citizens will be."

But if rituals are to be authentic, they must carry meaning beyond themselves. They must be the living out of the faith which the rituals both express and determine and not ends in themselves.

SQUEEZING IT IN WON'T WORK

Family worship is for families which have decided to make it a vital and integral part of their life, not something squeezed in. The family does not always have to come to grips with earthshaking problems of the world or even of the family. Family worship can be looking at the ordinary, the very stuff of life, that needs the added dimension of thoughtful and thankful living which recognizes the Giver of all life.

Dietrich Bonhoeffer, the German theologian martyred by the Nazis, outlines in *Life Together* the ritual of Christians who have the privilege of sharing life in a family:

Common life under the Word begins with common worship at the beginning of the day. The family community gathers for praise and thanks, reading of the Scriptures, and prayer. The deep stillness of morning is broken first by the prayer and song of the fellowship . . . . For Christians the beginning of the day should not be burdened and oppressed with besetting concerns for the day's work. At the threshold of the new day stands the Lord who made it . . . . Therefore, at the beginning of the day let all distraction and empty talk be silenced and let the first thought and the first word belong to him to whom our whole life belongs.

NO TWO ALIKE

Creativity in family worship is a must. The form it takes cannot be taken over from someone else. What is done must first of all fit your particular family, every member of it. This carries with it some "givens" for timing, length, repetition, and for playfulness partially determined by the ages of the children. Family worship should be lively, using so many forms of expression that each member is caught up in the feeling of anticipation and enjoyment. It should be a time of festivity—"We are happy to be together."

58

As A FaMiLY

Brighten It Up!

Upon rising fill the house with joyful music—popular records of "Morning Has Broken," "Here Comes the Sun," "I'd Like to Teach the World to Sing" or a hymn, "Joyful, Joyful We Adore Thee," "All Creatures of Our God and King."

Chanting is a form of communication that evokes feeling. It helps familiar scriptures take on new meaning. Each person stands with his feet about one foot apart and recites antiphonally or in unison while swaying slightly to the rhythm of the reading. After the initial self-consciousness has passed, adopt a unity of tone. Practice a few times. It is moving! As a starter try Psalm 23 in unison, Matthew 5:1-11 and Matthew 25:35-40 antiphonally.

The *beat of a drum* or any "instrument" in your home will add emphasis and variety. Beat out the rhythm of "In the beginning God created the heavens and the earth." Following the reading of the events of each day, accent "And there was evening and there was morning, one day." It is exciting to decide the appropriate times for "the beat."

Visualize a psalm. Psalm 104 is a tremendous visual psalm with its many pictures of nature: sky, clouds, moon. Psalms 148, 8, and 23 also speak of the natural world. Cut pictures from magazines to illustrate a psalm and make a montage of the psalm.

Prayers from newspapers give a new meaning to current events. Each person selects one article suggesting an item for prayer—one of concern or one of joy. Each member will read one important sentence from the article, followed by a moment of silence.

Make a prayer wall. Its design should be simple. Poster paper, wallboard, burlap, felt, or newsprint may be used. Decorate it according to the season.

Place the bulletin-board-type prayer wall in a well-traveled area of your home. Words such as asking, thanking, loving, caring may suggest elements of prayer. Let the wall "grow" as each member shares his ideas and as interest and concerns change.

You might include a snapshot of one in the family who is celebrating a birthday or a wedding, facing surgery or a long illness. Add a birth announcement, a notice of the death of a friend, a snip of fabric from a gown made for a prom. From time to time, post the schedule of an absent member, a blossom, a "turning" leaf, a quotation, or a symbol of achievement or promotion.

The list could go on and on, for— "The steadfast love of the Lord never ceases, his mercies never come to an end." Lamentations 3:22
Note: See the chapter "Poetry for Thanksgiving" for additional ideas.

Here is a prayer wall designed for use around Christmastime, with snippings of decorative greens from other rooms in the house.

What to Do on the Road

GETTING READY...

Take along play equipment in a bag or small box — one for each child. Include crayons, a packet of paper, pencils, blunt scissors, picture books. Stick in some shelf paper for making rubbings along the way. (See "Rubbings Revived.")

Games which you can rely upon to keep peace and quiet on the car trip abound. You will recall counting contests, memory and word games, spotting license plates and identifying cars which are old favorites.

James Barrie once wrote, "God gives us memory so that we may have roses in December." Why not plant them on your way to your vacation spot for travel is the gift of memories for the young!

Some think that travel is wasted on children, that they don't "get enough out of it" to warrant the cost and effort of taking them along. If you have this notion, just listen to the recollections of people who were fortunate enough to be taken along as children. Their minds are happily "washed" of memories of greasy food, uncomfortable beds, a flat tire — the sort of mundane incidents which so often color the whole experience for adults.

Instead children remember atmospheres and sensations, which they soak up like blotters — for that's how children are. Special sounds and scents, unaccustomed sights, the feel of the unfamiliar — these are the impressions that remain. The spine-chilling roar of Niagara Falls, the just-caught trout eaten in Colorado, the sound of raindrops on leaves at Cyprus Gardens, the ever-changing colors of a sunset on the plains, the antiphonal call of birds in the early morning—these are the childhood impacts which are cherished.

"PICKING YOUR BRAIN" GAMES

Have you heard of a badelyng of ducks? John Biggs in his song "Birds" lists twenty-two terms which describe birds in various groupings. A muster of peacocks, a nye of pheasants, a congregation of plovers, an exultation of larks. Did you know that a flock of geese in the air is called a skein of geese, but if they are on water or land, they are called a gaggle of geese?

Venture into the animal kingdom. What terms can your family recall?

Do you know the bird family with a baby called a cygnet, whose father is a cob and its mother a pen? A baby rabbit in its first year is a leveret. What is its mother called? Its father? You take it from here!

Tallahassee is the capital of Florida. Can you name the other forty-nine state capitals?

ELECTRONICS TO THE RESCUE!

If the trip will be a long one and you think games might become tiring, a tape recorder can save the day — going, at the destination, and upon return. Let the youngsters all announce what they hope to see, describe it as they see it, comment on it afterwards in those family sessions at the end of the day. They're usually satisfied to treat the recording process as a fun part of the day.

YOU'VE ARRIVED!

If your destination is by a lake or along a seacoast, you'll find that the beach is a good place to try some sand casting! You have most of what you need right there — a sandy beach, water (ocean water is all right), pebbles, shells, glass, a plastic pail for the water (a cut down bleach container is fine), and some plaster of Paris, which you will need to bring along.

• Dampen the sand, wetting it to "about the wetness of the beach after a wave has receded" but far enough away that a wave won't wipe out your creation.

• Form a concave shape, *packing the sand well*. Impressions may be made within the shape, using a spoon, your hands, a stick. Avoid very narrow areas which may break easily later.

• If mosaic is desired, put the pieces (pebbles, shells, other things you find) into the sand, pushing them in but leaving enough above the surface to catch in the plaster. The mosaic pieces should be facing down.

• When the shape and mosaic are complete, put water in the mixing pail and slowly pour in the plaster until it rises above the water. After it sets a minute, stir to remove any lumps, until it is the consistency of "good gravy." Carefully drizzle the mixture into the concave shape. (Caution: Do not use plaster after it has begun to thicken because it will not flow into the form well. If the solution is mixed too thinly to begin with, it will run under the mosaic pieces.)

If you wish to mount the casting, place a paper clip into the plaster.

• Let harden. Usually it takes about one or two hours for the plaster to set hard enough to remove without crumbling. Dig the sand away from the plaster shape. Remove the piece carefully and let dry for a while longer.

• The finished casting can be mounted on cork or wood backing, using the paper clip as a hook. Boards drifted upon the beach are appropriate in color and quality to bring out the best in the casting. Or, you might "distress" some pine or barn siding with a hammer when you get home and use it for the mounting board.

Besides the decorative pieces created, the total experience is rich in the "feeling of nature," which only results from becoming a part of "things" — the water, the sand, the materials found on the beach, the light, the air, the sun. . . .

"WHERE ARE WE?"

There's an Eloise, Florida, and a Wilbur, Colorado. You'll find Alice in Texas and Dale in West Virginia. Any names of people along your route?

How many words can you find in Chattahoochee, Pensacola, Bainbridge, or Andalusia, towns which you may go near on your vacation trip?

In Georgia, if you look quickly, you will see Opp; in Arizona, Ajo. List the "shortest" towns that you whiz by.

LET'S PLAY—

This is only an example. Any letter of the alphabet or any classification might be used.

	a	c	o	p
fruit			orange	
vegetable	avocado			
car		Chevy		
flower				
animal				porcupine

THE EYES HAVE IT

For eyes that are dim

"Would I wish to be young again? No, for I have learned too much to wish to lose it. . . . I am a far more valuable person today than I was 50 years ago, or 40 years ago, or 30, or 20 or even 10. I have learned so much since I was 70!" These are the words of Pearl Buck, now 79, who is at work on three major novels.

In "Essay on Life" in *Modern Maturity*, Miss Buck explains her reasoning. In earlier years one has to spend so much time learning the techniques of how to live happily. A newborn child has to learn to breathe, to cry, to eat, to sit up, to reach for, to walk, to talk.

Year by year each of us has to work

for techniques in order to master ourselves and reach a growing understanding of ourselves and others. Happiness, Miss Buck believes, is based on this primary understanding. We must understand ourselves before we can respect ourselves. We must respect ourselves before we can win the respect of others. We need both self-respect and the respect of others to achieve happiness. "It has been a wonderful experience," writes Miss Buck, "to learn to know myself — my capacities, my weaknesses, my likes and dislikes, the strengths and weaknesses of my body in which I am presently housed. It has been an absorbing study, a lifetime process which of course goes on endlessly."

Why don't those of you with years of experience in living record, by tape or cassette, some of the most memorable events in your life—the humorous incidents, the sad feelings, the joyous occasions, songs, or games? You might do this at a family gathering or when you just feel like reminiscing or philosophizing. Your family will be glad to hear "Grandma tell it like it was," and you will enjoy hearing yourself as you play it back.

For eyes with frames around them

"Where did you go?" "OUT" "What did you do?" "NOTHING" is the title of a book written by Robert Paul Smith in 1957. The antics described in it lead me to suspect that he was in that stage of life called middle-age. I chuckled my way through much of the book because it recalled many familiar experiences.

In the summer, there were long evenings under the street lamps to watch the big kids talk to girls, to sit on the porch and listen to the "old folks" talk politics. It was the time to find a jelly glass and to fill it full of lightning bugs and to see, when it got very dark, that your finger, where you touched the lightning bug, glowed too.

Seasons also determined what you played. There was a time you played immies if you were a boy and skip the rope if you were a girl. Girls didn't play marbles and boys didn't jump rope. There was a time you played stoop ball. There was a time when you built kites. Everybody did it. As Mr. Smith explains it, "There was something that clicked and gears shifted and we all got up in the morning and put our immies in our pockets because that was the day everybody started to play immies."

Spring always meant radishes and green onions from the garden. The Fourth of July, fried chicken. Corn on the cob came later in the summer. Some things were not eaten together like pickles and milk. You believed, but really knew better, that grasshoppers spit tobacco and that if you stepped on a crack you would break your mother's back. Dad watched the newly-sprouted

corn, hoping it would be knee high by the 4th and Mom's decision to hang out the weekly wash was determined by "Rain before seven; quit before eleven."

When nothing more exciting was going, you sucked water through a licorice stick, caught tadpoles, played in the mud, learned to whistle and snap your fingers, looked at the sky which was full of animals that seemed to float, swoop, and swim in the air, or you just stretched out in the backyard and chewed grass, made clover bracelets, or curled dandelion stems with your tongue. There seemed to be nothing wrong about doing nothing.

"These days," writes Mr. Smith, "you see a kid lying on his back and looking blank and you begin to wonder what's wrong with him. There's nothing wrong with him, except he's thinking. He's trying to find out whether he breathes differently when he's thinking about it than when he's just breathing. He's seeing how long he can sit there without blinking. He is considering whether his father is meaner than Carl's father, he is wondering who he would be if his father hadn't married his mother, whether there is somewhere in the world somebody who is exactly like him in every detail. . . ."

Sometimes we must admit that we were bored when we were young. But to do nothing is not the same as to be bored. Being bored is something we let happen to us when we are doing nothing.

How long has it been since your wrists were red from playing scissors-paperstone? Have you played Ante-Ante-Over lately? Do you remember how to play "Wire, briar, limber locks — ten geese in one flock?" Gossip? Have you taught your kids how to play Button, Button or Hide the Thimble? When did you last pop corn, eat cold, crisp, juicy delicious apples, or pull taffy? Have you taken time to look at the flowers, trees, insects, and people with the same awe you did when you were 6 or 8? Have you played Fox and Geese in the snow? Statues?

Where did you say you were going? Out? What are you going to do? Just sit on the back steps and watch the grass grow!

For eyes that dance with anticipation

Before days of do-it-yourself kits and when the ready-made toys were very expensive, you used the things around you, applied your imagination and skill, and made your own toys. Here are directions for three funny little things I enjoyed as a kid. I hope you will enjoy them, too. They are toys which your father or grandfather may remember making.

A spool tractor

You will need a thread spool (a large one is best but any will do), a rubber band, a candle or soft soap (such as Ivory), two kitchen matches. From the soap or candle cut a disc about ¼″ thick and smaller than the end of the spool. Make a small hole in the center. (It takes a bit of patience and skill to keep from breaking the soap or candle.)

Break off the ends of the matches, making one about 2″ long; the other about 1″. (These will vary with the size of the spool, a part of your experimenting.) Cut a small groove on either side of the hole on one end of the spool. Thread the rubber band through the hole, insert the smallest match through the loop and slip into the groove. Now, thread the disc onto the other end of the rubber band and insert the larger matchstick in that loop. Your spool tractor is ready to go. Wind up its rubber-band motor by turning the longer matchstick. Place on a smooth surface and watch it go!

To make a climber out of the tractor, notch the wheels (ends of the spool) with tiny grooves. Make a hump in a scatter rug and up the hill it will climb. Experiment with your tractor until it's as efficient as you can make it, then sug-

Here are components for making a spool tractor. For fun, we decorated ours with flowers in bright tempera colors

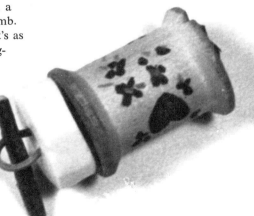

gest a race with another tractor. Or, place two tractors together (head on) and see which is the stronger.

A small nail or two small nails may be used instead of the small matchstick, and a bead may be substituted for the disc of soap or candle, but some of the fun is in the experimenting. The "sophistication" takes away part of this experience.

Buzz-saw buttons

These little hummers are made by passing a nylon string through two holes of a very large button. (Hope you can find one in these days of the zipper!) Tie the ends of the thread together. Wind up the string by twirling the two ends in your hands — round and round. Now, pull the string out and the button will look and sound like a buzz-saw. After pulling the hands apart, relax them and let the string rewind itself before stretching it out again. It works on the same principle as a yo-yo. There's an art to it — so keep experimenting until you're an expert "buzz-saw operator."

For a more sophisticated toy, cut a ⅛″ hardboard disc with a jig saw, 3, 2½ or 2″ in diameter. Drill two holes in the disc about ½-1″ apart. Drill two holes in two ⅜″ dowel pins for handles. Thread string through handles and disc. Pull the handles and the disc spins and hums.

A handkerchief parachute

Tie four one-foot lengths of string to the corners of a handkerchief. Gather the free string ends and tie in a knot about 4″ from bottom. For the weight, use a stone or some metal washers. Add the amount of weight to make the parachute float gently to the ground after its toss into the air. A parachute has to be "packed" just right for its descent to be smooth and strings remain untangled. Happy landing! □

INDEX